SHUT UP! NOBODY LIKES YOU

DREW KELECHI

CONTENTS

INTRODUCTION

ARE YOU WHITE OR BLACK?

Why do I have these stupid-looking teeth? Only strange Africans have a gap between their front teeth. It makes me look like a walking joke every time I open my mouth. And why is my hair so kinky?

Sometimes I pulled my annoying hair between my index fingers and thumbs, then I pressed it against my forehead, trying desperately to straighten it. I became enraged when it instantly sprang back into its naturally tight coil.

I watched all the other kids at school shaking their majestic manes back and forth, their silky, straight hair sweeping across their faces. *Why can't I be cool like that?* The other kids combed their hair with long, clean strokes. I couldn't do that. I had to shove a comb into my hair, repeatedly pulling the hair from my scalp to make it gradually enlarge into an odd, circular sponge. It really hurt when they caught me using a hair pick.

"What are you doing, Drew?" they asked.

What does that question even mean?! *I'm combing my hair.* But of course I quickly hid the comb in my pocket so as not to draw attention to myself. "Nothing," I mumbled.

"Drew, are you white or black?" they asked me.

"I'm just Drew," I responded weakly.

I just want to fit in and have friends. Why is it so hard for them to accept me? It's not my fault I'm ugly.

Daddy was an albino from Nigeria, and Mommy was Caucasian from America. Looking so "odd" made it hard for me to be a kid. The judgments of my peers were swift and severe. There was no forgiveness.

Why do people seem so eager to hate each other?

1

YOU'RE NOT INVITED

I scanned the street left and right for sign of the ice cream truck, my ears occasionally picking up its carnival melodies. I'd spent the last ninety minutes with a stick in my hand, savagely beating the tall oak tree in our front yard, which I fought every day in epic lightsaber duels—all part of an active imagination. There were plenty of other kids on my block, but that tree was my only consistent playmate.

"Drew, what are you doing?! What's wrong with you?!" shouted Ms. Rita from next door.

My heart sank, and butterflies fluttered in the pit of my stomach.

"Don't you know that you're stripping the tree of all its bark?" added Ms. Rita, frowning at me. "You're gonna kill it!"

"I'm sorry, Ms. Rita," I replied.

"No you're not!" she snapped "You hit that tree every day. Why don't you find some kids to play with instead?"

I kept quiet. Ms. Rita always told her children to stay away from me. I could tell she hated me. Whenever her daughter, Tara, wandered across their lawn and onto our driveway, her mother yelled through their living room window, "Tara, come here please!" Then Tara would disappear for the day.

Posing after hitting the tree with sticks

Daddy let me get ice cream once a week. I knew this would be the third time in seven days, but I thought maybe I could persuade him. When I saw the roof of the ice cream truck at the top of our street, I threw my saber to the ground and sprinted up the hill. I suddenly crashed to the cement, injuring my knee badly. But the adrenaline shifted my focus back to what was really important: ice cream.

Getting back up, I continued to run. I wore an insane grin plastered across my sunburned face when I reached the ice cream truck. Oh no! I hadn't brought any money...but the truck was only at the first house. Surely there would be time for me to run home and return before he was gone for good.

"I'll be right back, sir!" I yelled to the ice cream man. My excitement carried me halfway down the hill before I crashed to the cement a second time. The neighbors looked at me with a mixture of disgust and hatred. I scampered up the porch stairs to Daddy, blood dripping down both of my legs. I begged him for ice cream money. Calling me hyper would be an understatement, but then I was only five years old.

Tanner was a white boy who lived up the street and went to God's Lamb, the same elementary school I attended. We were in the same kindergarten class. Tanner's father, Billy, was from Louisiana, and his mother, Anna May, was from a part of Alabama where they didn't take kindly to Black folks. At the time our families met, I was the only boy in the neighborhood Tanner's age. Plus our parents went to the same church, so I became Tanner's playmate by default.

Tanner and I loved to duel with his plastic swords, but he always aimed his blows at my face. I thought it was normal roughhousing, but my father recognized a dark trend: I bled almost every time we played together. Daddy told me not to let Tanner hit my face, and he had to visit Tanner's house often to talk with Mr. Billy about his son's carelessness. Apparently those discussions fell upon deaf ears, but I wouldn't know any of that until much later.

For the week before Tanner's sixth birthday party, all the kids at school were talking about it. They said he was going to have inflatable bounce houses, a magician, and tons of delicious food. I'd been thinking long and hard about what kind of gift to get him. I knew he loved swords, but he had enough of those. A dart gun? Yeah, he would absolutely love that. I couldn't wait to see the elation on his face when he unwrapped the greatest gift imaginable. I'd be his best friend after that!

The day before Tanner's party, I was dribbling a soccer ball on our front lawn when I heard someone yell, "Hey, Drew!" I looked up the street and saw Tanner standing on his front porch.

"Hey, Tanner. You wanna play?" I shouted back excitedly.

"Guess what? I'm having a birthday party tomorrow, and you're not invited!" he yelled, his face gleeful.

I couldn't believe my ears. I was absolutely devastated. I ran inside and tearfully told Mommy and Daddy of Tanner's cutting words. They tried to comfort me, but that didn't work.

Why didn't he want me to come to his party?

There had to be some kind of explanation. Maybe there had been some sort of misunderstanding.

"Mommy, maybe he was just kidding," I sobbed. "I wanna go talk to him. There's just no way he was serious."

"Honey, don't worry," she purred kindly. "Stay inside with us, and let's play a board game."

Daddy rubbed my back and hugged me. "Don't cry, my baby. You are going to be a great success."

I didn't care what I was going to be. I only cared that I was missing out on Tanner's party. I'd known Tanner for such a long time. How could this be happening? Why didn't he want me to be his best friend?

I'd only seen Aunt Candace in photos, but I always admired her. She was my only aunt who had long, flowing blonde hair. On top of that, I remember Mommy talking fondly of the fun they shared as teenagers. One morning, I was eating my breakfast at the kitchen table when the phone rang.

"I got it," I yelled, picking up the line.

"Hi, this is your aunt, Candace. Is your mother around?" she said.

My heart began to pound. I'd never heard her voice before. I froze for a moment, before saying, "Yes, she is, Aunt Candace."

"Well that's good news. May I speak with her please?" Her voice sounded distant and artificially cheerful.

"I'll get her for you." For some reason, I was beginning to panic. I'd tried my best to hold a conversation with her, but I couldn't think of anything interesting or important to say. Maybe if I had sounded cool enough, she would have asked to talk with me. I felt like I'd blown my one chance to impress her.

Aunt Candace had lived in the same city we'd lived in my whole life, but she was an extremely busy lady. So busy, in fact, that we'd never once met in person. I figured that was just how it was when you're a grownup with an important job. Some days I wondered why I'd met all of Daddy's Black brothers but none of Mommy's white siblings.

After Mommy got off the phone, I learned some exciting news: Aunt Candace was hosting a party at Grandma Lucy's house! I'd finally get to hang out with her! We could draw together, toss the Frisbee, and maybe even play street hockey!

"Mommy, I'm bringing the hockey sticks!" I shouted, unable to contain my joy.

"Actually, honey, we have a babysitter coming over to watch you," Mommy said.

I felt like I'd been punched in the belly. This was way

worse than being excluded from Tanner's party. "Why, Mommy? I wanna see Aunt Candace," I protested. "I promise I'll behave myself."

Mommy rubbed my back. "This is an adult party, sweetheart. Children aren't allowed."

Between my mommy and her two sisters, I was the only child in the family. So having an adult-only party just meant *Drew* wasn't welcome to the family event.

I found out years later that there was a reason that we never saw Aunt Candace. The truth was that she'd spent her entire life degrading my mother, who has always had the most forgiving and loving heart. Growing up, Candace posted pictures all over the house of herself with her friends, but she made sure that my mother was never included in any of them. Candace always refused to take pictures with her. She made fun of Mommy's "poofy" hair. She also viciously ridiculed Mommy whenever she bought or received something of value.

"Why did you get that?" Candace demanded. "You don't need something like that!"

Their parents never stopped Candace from ridiculing my mother because Candace was the golden child. My mother was the neglected middle child, who suffered regular abuse from each member of the family.

On school days, when they were in a rush to get to class, Candace intentionally locked my mother out of the bathroom, preventing her from getting ready and making her late for school. And when they were in high school, their parents urged Candace to go to Princeton, but they told Mommy that she should be a secretary.

Aunt Candace's first marriage was to a doctor. They always made sure to invite family and friends to their gatherings, but they never included my mother or father, who were shunned because they were an interracial couple. I learned that Candace frequently drove from her county to Virginia Beach to vacation with her friend, and she had to pass through our city in Maryland. Not once did she invite my mother.

My father had one other brother living in the United States at the time. His name was Uncle Akachi. My father's four other brothers lived in various parts of the world, including Russia, Rwanda, and Nigeria, where their mother also lived. I'd known Uncle Akachi since I was a baby, and he'd always taken care of me like I was his first son. On occasion, I got to spend the weekend with him at his house, where we ate butter pecan ice cream and watched cartoons together. Uncle also had a very cool collection of action movies, and although Mommy and Daddy forbade me from watching rated-R movies, Uncle Akachi never stopped me from sliding them into the VCR and marveling at the explosions and fight scenes.

Whenever Mommy and Daddy had a family get together, I always looked forward to Uncle Akachi coming over because he played soccer with me or orchestrated some other fascinating adventure, like letting me steer his car up and down our driveway as he monitored the gas and brake pedal. He was the best uncle a young boy could ask for. He was also the only family member who bothered to attend our events. Unfortunately, Uncle Akachi's work forced him to move to Georgia later that year. That was heartbreaking for me.

Unlike Uncle Akachi, Aunt Candace *always* had something more important to do than to come to our house to see me. My white grandmother, Lucy, who lived in a nearby county, wasn't much better. Nine times out of ten, she told my mother that it wasn't the right day for her to come over to our house because she had plans with her friends. Only very rarely did Grandma Lucy take the time to visit us, and whenever she did, it was never for longer than ninety minutes.

Grandma Lucy hadn't wanted my parents to get married, and when she initially learned of my father's race when he first started dating my mother, she nearly disowned her daughter. Eventually, Grandma Lucy had to come to terms with the fact that Mommy and Daddy weren't going to separate, and they might even decide to get married. That wasn't easy for her to accept. When my mother happily announced to her family that she was going to marry my father, she encountered less resentment, although they still didn't congratulate her.

At the time, my parents were extremely poor, so Lucy made a promise to buy my mother's wedding dress. But the week of their wedding, Lucy told my mother that she wouldn't be purchasing the dress after all, nor would she attend the wedding because she planned to go on vacation with one of her childhood friends that week. On their wedding day, none of my mother's family members showed up.

In spite of the slights, my parents still had the spirit of forgiveness in their hearts, so even after the wedding catastrophe, they kept in contact with Lucy. But a few years later, when my parents announced that they would be having their first child, Lucy's reception was lukewarm. And she became downright hostile at times. Once, while my parents were visiting Lucy's house when my mother was pregnant, my father, grinning, called her Grandma. She exploded in a fit of anger, warning him that her name was Lucy and nothing more.

Months later, my mother went into labor early. My father had called Lucy to come to the hospital, but she told him that she had errands to run and couldn't make it. My sister, Sarah, was born in an emergency C-section delivery. She was alarmingly premature. Baby Sarah couldn't breathe on her own, and several other complications concerned her doctors. They took her to intensive care while my mother struggled to stay conscious. Sarah was alive for eight hours before she went back to heaven. The doctors didn't want to tell my mother the news too soon because it likely would have had a catastrophic effect on her mental state.

Eventually, my mother climbed out of her hospital bed and limped to the neonatal intensive care unit in search of her daughter. The nurses were alerted and guided her to a room, where they broke the horrific news to her. My mother collapsed.

My parents stayed in the hospital for a few more days, but not once did Lucy call.

A few years later, I showed up. I was a twin, but six weeks into the pregnancy, my mother lost the other baby. She had to stay in bed for nine months because she was high risk and prone to complications. That wasn't easy for her and my father, who were living out of an attic. My mother went to live with Lucy in her suburban rancher-style home, which was lavish and sprawling. What should have been a relaxing, mother-daughter bonding period was an excruciating masterclass on shunning. If Lucy wasn't complaining that my mother was being needy, she was grousing that she was using too much toilet paper or that she was sleeping too many hours every night. The relentless, mean-spirited criticism and accusations left my mother weary and terribly depressed. Lucy constantly showed her annoyance with my mother in the most passive aggressive of ways, but the message was clear: my mother was an unwanted burden.

On bedrest under her doctor's orders, my mother was unable to provide meals for herself. She had to beg her mother for food, which was delivered only reluctantly. Lucy treated my mother worse than the average person treats a sick dog. It was overt exclusion. Lucy excluded my mother from conversations. She excluded my mother from gatherings. My mother learned about get togethers that Lucy hosted only when she heard the footsteps of guests from her bedroom.

My parents kept me away from Tanner for about a week, all the while teaching me the importance of forgiveness. They told me that an angry heart would lead to a tainted mind. After the party, I found out that one of Tanner's birthday gifts was a new bike with training wheels. It was so fancy, with its chrome frame and colorful stickers. I was surprisingly excited for him when he rode it up our driveway a few days later.

"Wow, cool bike, Tanner!" I gushed.

He shrugged. "Yeah, I know. My dad bought it for me at the party, so it's mine and not yours."

I paused, trying to think of an appropriate response. "Ok, well it looks really neat with all those stickers."

"Yup, I know. I put them on all by myself," said Tanner.

He rolled down the sidewalk and into the street, then he looped back into our driveway.

"Hey, Tanner. You think I can have a turn when you're done?" I asked.

He looked uncertain. "Umm...I don't know. I guess. Maybe," he replied.

"Cool! Thanks a lot, Tanner."

Surprisingly, he stepped off the bike and rolled it toward me. I carefully mounted the seat. The pedals had only made a few revolutions when a high-pitched wail startled me. I looked back at Tanner. Big crocodile tears were running down his cheeks. Petrified, I watched as he ran back up the street to his father, who was standing on their front porch, his arms akimbo, looking stern.

"What's wrong?" his father shouted.

"Andrew won't give me my bike back," Tanner moaned.

"Then you go get your damn bike back from him!" he bellowed.

I was dumbfounded. I didn't know what to do or what to say. I tried to explain that I'd politely asked Tanner for a turn on his new bike and that I never would have taken it from him because that's not nice behavior, and that hurts people's feelings.

I had no idea why Tanner was telling his father that I wouldn't give the bike back, but before Tanner had stepped off his driveway, I'd already stepped off his bike and backed away, afraid of what he might do to me.

I rushed into the house and told Daddy the entire story. He promised to buy me my own bike that evening. Within an hour, we were walking up and down the bike isle at our local toy store. I picked out a big, red bike with black mountain bike tires and a set of removable training wheels. I was beyond thrilled.

When we got back home, there was still enough daylight to ride in front of our house. My heart raced with excitement as we unloaded my bike from the car, and as soon as the tires hit our driveway, I was pedaling madly.

"Come back and get your helmet," Daddy warned.

"Yes, Daddy," I replied.

As I rode my new bike, Daddy smiled from our front porch. I could tell that he was very proud of me.

Not ten minutes after we got home, Tanner wandered down the sidewalk to our side of the street. Standing at the foot of our driveway, he stared at me.

"Is that a new bike?" he eventually asked.

I had no malice in my heart, and I honestly couldn't understand his behavior. "Yes, Tanner. This is my new bike."

"Can I try it?" he asked.

I couldn't believe my ears. How in the world did he think it was okay to ask for a turn on my new bike after lying to his father while I rode his? Bewildered, I looked across the lawn to the front porch, where Daddy sat with an expression on my face that seemed to say, *Are you hearing what I am hearing?*

But without hesitation, Daddy said, "Go ahead, son. Let him ride."

I motioned for Tanner to come get the bike. He sprang on it and pedaled the bike up the hill to his house, where his father was reclining in a chair on the front lawn.

"Hey, look at this bike, Dad! It's Drew's."

His father threw his hands up, as if to say, *Big deal.*

In spite of my efforts that year, my relationship with Tanner deteriorated. So I found another playmate who was three years younger than I was. His name was Chris. Our favorite game was called "tackle." It involved wrestling each other in the grass and mimicking the moves we watched on WWE. Sometimes we dug deep holes in the dirt, and other times we crashed our toy trucks into each other and marvel at the destruction. We had so much fun outside, but we never played inside my house. His parents had told him that he could never step foot in our home. Unbeknownst to me, they hated everything about me. Mommy and Daddy had warned me to stay away from Chris and his family, but I didn't have the patience or willpower to play by myself every day.

A few months after we started playing together, everybody in the neighborhood but me received an invitation to his birthday party. I only found out about it through one of the kids down the street. I guessed that they must have forgotten to send my invitation.

On the day of the party, Daddy instructed me to stay away from Chris' house because they clearly didn't want me there. But how could I ignore the shrieks of kids having the time of their lives right up the street? Once again, I disobeyed him and wandered up the street. I ended up in Chris' backyard. As I stepped onto their property, I realized that nobody was greeting me or even acknowledging my presence.

Naturally, I ran up to a group of kids playing some sort of hand game. They all stopped and stared at me, but I didn't think anything of it. I wandered to the food table, where Chris' mother was serving punch.

"Good afternoon, Ms. Anna May. Please, may I have some punch?" I was only a foot away from her, but she seemed not to have heard me. So I asked her a second time if she didn't mind serving me punch.

Ms. Anna May shouted in the general direction of the yard, "Has everybody been served punch yet?"

I stood there, awestruck. I didn't understand why she was ignoring me. I was too embarrassed to ask a third time, so I hung my head. Right then, she yanked the plastic cup from my hands and half filled it with punch. She made me feel so small.

Holding that cup of punch, I walked home, wondering what I might have done to offend Ms. Anna May. Had I been rude to her? When I walked into our house, my father was wearing an exasperated expression in the living room. I explained to him what had happened, and he became very angry. He told me that he'd warned me not to venture over to Chris' house. He was livid that I'd defied him. I apologized and told him that I wouldn't do it again.

Holding newborn Micah

That year, my brother, Micah, was born. It was amazing to have a companion in the house, even if he was only a baby and couldn't play with me yet. I loved him so much and couldn't wait until he was old enough to play catch with a football or to pass a soccer ball back and forth. It was always so painful looking out the window, watching all the other children in the neighborhood running around together. I wished I had the power to speed up time. I wanted Micah to be a big boy so I could finally have a play-mate who wasn't mean to me.

2

YOU DON'T HAVE TO PLAY WITH HIM

By the time I was eight years old, Ms. Anna May had spread word in our surrounding communities that everyone should stay away from the "troubled" mixed boy. She completely alienated me from the other kids in the neighborhood. It became increasingly painful to live there. Even the kids who had recently moved to our block kept away from our house.

One day, when I was wallowing in my loneliness, I heard the distinct sound of a skateboard coming from down the street. My curious eyes found a talented teenager maneuvering his way around a cul-de-sac, doing tricks I'd never even imagined were possible. At first, I just stood there and watched quietly as he flipped the board, landed perfectly back on top, then skated off into another direction. Not once did he acknowledge my presence, but I understood that it was because he was engrossed. He looked so cool! His hair was dyed blonde, but I could just make out his brown roots. He rode around shirtless, his pants sagging.

After about five minutes of watching in awe, I bravely spoke. "Hello, my name's Drew."

"Sup," he said, flipping his chin up at me. He kept riding the whole time.

Wow! This guy's awesome! I thought. For some reason, I had a feeling that he didn't want to be bothered, so I didn't try engaging him in further conversation.

Plink! His board hit the rail that he'd set up about twenty feet from where I stood. His board slid effortlessly to the end of the rail, then he jumped and spun 180 degrees. Somehow his board stayed glued to the bottom of his feet as he landed perfectly on the ground. I was hypnotized.

He landed hardflips with incredible ease (I learned skater-speak in the coming months). He did a 360 Indy off of his funbox and transferred to a rail on a tailslide grind just as easily as you would walk down the sidewalk. He skated toward one of his ramps, this time coming in from a different angle. I could see from the intensity in his eyes that he was about to attempt something very difficult. He shot off the ramp, flipped his board under him, and caught it in the air. But as he was approaching the landing, his back wheels skidded to the side, and he sprawled out on the pavement. He screamed obscenities. He had a serious temper, but I'd soon learn that was very much encouraged in skateboarding culture.

I found out that his name was Tim, and he was the first person I idolized. I began obsessing over the cool white dudes in the *SkateLife* magazine. They were professional skaters who had their pictures taken as they used their skateboards to jump from rooftop to rooftop or down an entire flight of stairs. But Mommy wouldn't let me read the magazine due to an inordinate number of curse words. Whenever we went to our local supermarket, I wandered off to the magazine section and picked up the latest issue, then I got back into the cart. I remember trying so hard to sneak it onto the conveyor belt when we were checking out, but Mommy was always way too sharp for such shenanigans.

"Put it back," she demanded, her brows knit. I could never get anything past Mommy.

That summer, Mommy and Daddy purchased a piano, and they told me that I needed to practice every day. They gave me $1 every day I practiced piano, which meant that I typically had close to $30 by the end of the month. They also signed me up for Camp Red Feather, which was hosted at McLan, one of the nicest private schools in Maryland. McLan, which was grades K–12, boasted 750 acres of beautiful land that afforded students opportunities to do activities like horseback riding. They had four swimming pools, three gigantic gymnasiums, and countless sports fields. Mommy was absolutely dedicated to giving me the best possible childhood, and she saw McLan as a place for me to do the things that I couldn't do in my emotionally toxic neighborhood. I was part of a soccer team that met two or three times a week for games and practices, but that wasn't enough to protect me from my neighbors.

As I boarded the McLan bus in the morning, the distinct smell of diesel and fruit-scented sunscreen told me that I was going someplace special. Mommy and Daddy always told me to sit in the front of the bus to avoid trouble, but the front was boring. The back was where you could yell all you wanted and jump extra high if your timing was just right when the bus drove over a speed bump. You also had the freedom to switch benches without the bus driver barking at you to have a seat as we snaked down Baltimore County backroads.

When we got to McLan, our first activity of the day was arts and crafts in the lower school—the fancy way of saying "elementary school"—which I liked very much. My creations always drew considerable attention. I would find out later that they thought I had some artistic talent. Next, we ventured out into the woods to complete obstacle courses, where hidden puzzle pieces were strewn about. We had to collect them all so we could complete our morning challenge. Once finished, we reconvened in the lower school building for lunch.

After we ate, we made our way back to the stables across campus for horseback riding. Being so close to such a large animal left me in awe, and it was one of the main attractions of Camp Red Feather for me. But nothing beat swimming to escape the heat of the summer. We swam right after horseback riding, and we were usually exhausted afterward. We got a quick snack after swimming, then we lay down for nap time. After a nap, we had a final free period, when we were allowed to let loose on the massive playground. It was during one of these free periods that I had my first traumatizing encounter with a larger Black boy.

Tyrell stood about a foot taller than I was, and he was playing basketball with a bunch of big eleven-year-olds on the opposite side of the court. On my side, an Indian kid and I had been shooting the ball for a few minutes before Tyrell came up to us.

"Ayo, light-bright—we gonna use this whole court, so it's time for you to scram for real," he said to me.

I was taken aback by the animosity in his voice, but I still responded like a gentleman. "How about we all play together?"

"I don't think you wanna do that, but suit yourself," he scoffed. His body language was threatening.

He divided everybody into teams, then the game began. Tyrell got the ball and charged me as he dribbled furiously toward the lowered hoop on our side of the court. As he passed me, he stomped on my foot as hard as he could and scored a basket. I wondered if he'd meant to hurt me. I guessed by the scowl on his face and his clenched teeth that he had. But then maybe that was just his game face. I decided to let it roll off my back. But a minute later, Tyrell stepped up his aggression. As I stood near the basket, attempting to defend it, he leapt into the air to dunk the ball. His elbow landed directly on the top of my skull as he came back to the ground. I yelled in pain and grabbed my head, stumbling off the court. As I walked away, I could hear him and his friends laughing and jeering. "Yeah, that's what your little light-skinned butt gets. I told you this was my house, country boy."

I reported to one of the counselors and decided to stay inside until dismissal.

Aside from that encounter, my days at McLan were typically amazing because I actually had the opportunity to interact with children my age. I also loved seeing Mommy's smiling face waiting to pick me up from the bus stop at the end of the day. But then we would turn down our street, and I heard the shrieks of children playing in my neighborhood, and my heart sank. I remembered that I was the unwanted boy. *Why don't they want me to have water gun battles with them?* I thought, tears welling up in my eyes.

There was still daylight left after we got home from camp, so I went out skateboarding. Within a few weeks, I could maneuver my way across our driveway and down the street without stepping off the skateboard. Skating grew into a new passion, especially as I watched Tim's jaw-dropping acrobatics at the bottom of our street every day.

Skateboarding near Tim

Aunt Candace had just recently remarried after a tumultuous divorce, and she relocated to Pennsylvania. Toward the end of the summer, Mommy told me that she and I were going to visit Aunt Candace at her new house. *We're gonna have so much fun playing games together!* I hoped I'd be able to impress her so she'd want to visit us sometime in the near future.

We arrived at Aunt Candace's brand-new mansion after a two-hour drive. I got to ring the doorbell. A short, heavyset man opened the door and greeted my mother. I learned that he was my new uncle, Greg. I extended my hand and shook his. He stooped down and greeted baby Micah, who was now three years old. Greg seemed like a pretty nice guy. He led us into their enormous foyer.

"Where's Candace?" Mommy asked Uncle Greg.

"Oh, she's on the phone with one of her friends. She should be downstairs soon," he replied.

We sat with him in the living room for twenty minutes, making small talk and joking back and forth. I began to think to myself that maybe Aunt Candace hadn't heard the doorbell ring and that maybe she was unaware of our arrival. But the truth was that Aunt Candace was intentionally keeping us waiting to show us how meaningless we were.

A few more minutes passed before I heard someone slowly making their way down the stairs. Aunt Candace had a fake grin plastered across her face. Mommy got up and hugged her emphatically. I stood behind them, awaiting my turn.

"How are you, Drew?" she asked.

"Fine, thank you," I replied. "I'm so happy to see you Auntie! I brought some really fun games I think you might enjoy."

She chuckled condescendingly. "Oh, today isn't much of a game day, honey."

I froze. *Maybe she's in a bad mood.* I thought. *Maybe she isn't feeling well.*

Aunt Candace motioned for us to follow her, and she gave us a tour of her new home. "Drew, don't touch anything, and make sure your little brother doesn't either," she warned as she led us to the kitchen.

I began to feel uncomfortable, but I forced out of my head the idea that we weren't welcome after all.

We saw a few more rooms before I wandered back to the living room, where I'd left the backpack that contained my handheld video games and a football. I pulled the ball out of my bag and found Uncle Greg. I asked him if he wanted to play catch.

"Sure, buddy. Let's do it," he responded.

I followed him out to the backyard, tingling with excitement. *I bet Uncle Greg is good at catch!* I handed him the ball, sprinted to the middle of their spacious lawn, my hands out in front of me. He launched a perfect spiral pass directly to me. I effortlessly caught the ball.

"Nice catch!" he yelled.

This day couldn't have turned out any more perfect. I threw a bullet pass back to him.

"Good throw, Drew!"

Not five minutes later, Aunt Candace appeared on the back porch with a look of disdain on her face. "Greg, what are you doing?" she barked.

"Honey, we're just having a little bonding time. Drew's quite the athlete!" he responded.

"Yeah, that's great, but you don't have to play with him for long," she said.

"I know, honey," Greg responded.

I was shocked. *Did I do something to anger Aunt Candace? Why's she being so mean?* I shifted side to side nervously, dreading the moment he'd say that it was time to call it quits.

Sure enough, eight throws after Aunt Candace went inside, Uncle Greg said, "All right, pal. Time's up."

I felt like saying to him, *Why so soon? We haven't even been out here for ten minutes*, but the truth was I'd just met him, and that wouldn't be polite.

That familiar feeling of overwhelming loneliness swept over me as Greg left me outside in the yard by myself.

3

YOU FRIZZY-HEADED FREAK

King's Hall was an elite all-boys private school for children who were extra smart or who were from affluent families. I was the only child in my grade who didn't have super-rich parents, and I was very rarely invited for playdates or birthday parties. Still, I was grateful to have a place where I could escape our toxic neighborhood. I'd been at the school since kindergarten, learning new things and taking piano lessons once a week.

I was so proud when I started my third grade year. I remember feeling so mature as I logged all my homework into my daily agenda so I wouldn't miss any assignments. King's Hall challenged its students in all academic areas, and it was no place for slouches. They made that clear to us every day.

In the mornings before I left for school, I always made sure I had the appropriate vocabulary books and journals so that I wouldn't face scrutiny from my teachers. I didn't have any problems with the teachers or any of the other faculty members because they thought I was an intelligent boy and an avid learner. I excelled academically, but my favorite class was PE because I could let loose. The other students thought of me as the most athletic student in the entire lower school, and when it came time to choose teams for any sport, my peers quarreled over me, making me feel valuable and special for the first time in my life.

My one problem was that I became a class clown that year. I craved validation, and my classmates' laughter at my antics gave me a feeling of pure euphoria. Although my silliness disrupted class and resulted in reprimands from certain teachers, the immediate rush of affirmation from my peers outweighed the occasional trips to the principal's office. My behavior really wasn't that bad. Several other boys in my class were far more disruptive than I was.

Some of teachers showed me kindness and compassion, but a few of them showed obvious disdain for me. And I *felt it.* I was one of only two Black children in an entire lower school, which had 200 kids. In the minds of some teachers there, I'm sure I fit the stereotype of the uncontrollable Black boy with behavioral issues. When a teacher who disliked me passed by me in the hall, I felt a negative presence that hit me like I was walking into a storm cloud.

Mrs. Taylor, the lower school science teacher, was one of those teachers. My classmates and I sometimes joked around in her class, but we were careful not to be disrespectful when she was talking. Sometimes, though, we couldn't hold back uncontrollable giggles, especially when one of us whispered a joke about poo and pee. If two of the other white class clowns began giggling, Mrs. Taylor might look up from her desk and give them a stern look, but her reaction to me was very different.

If I started laughing, Mrs. Taylor would scream, "Would you like to leave the class, you crazy animal?!"

She scared me back into my senses. When she spoke with me, she seemed to have a heart of ice. I couldn't understand why.

I remember one day in particular when she made me feel terrible. It was a Tuesday morning, and everyone in homeroom was looking forward to science next period because the baby chicks in our class incubator had hatched the previous day. That meant that we were going to hold and feed them that day, and I couldn't wait.

When we arrived at science class, Mrs. Taylor took roll call and announced, "All right boys, today is the big day! Our baby chicks have hatched, and you know what that means."

My classmates and I cheered enthusiastically.

"We'll be learning a lot about these cute little critters, and you'll remember this experience for the rest of your lives," Mrs. Taylor continued. "So now I need you all to sit on the carpet, and I'll bring them over to you." She paused and looked at everyone in the class but me. "Except for

Drew. He doesn't get to participate today because he thought it was a good idea to be a class clown yesterday."

My chest burned, and I suddenly felt dizzy, as if I'd entered a dream state.

"Drew, get out of my classroom!" she bellowed.

"But, Mrs. Taylor, I'm sorry for—"

"GET OUT!" she shouted at the top of her lungs.

I mechanically rose to my feet and stumbled toward the door. I couldn't feel my legs. The tears I was trying to choke back seemed about to explode through my stinging eyes, my ears, my mouth, and my nose all at once. As I left the room, Mrs. Taylor slammed the door with all her might, which momentarily made me forget my urge to cry. Instead, I was frightened.

As I sat outside her classroom, I told myself that she'd eventually let me back in to play with the chicks. Five minutes passed, then ten, then fifteen. I was in total denial, telling myself that she couldn't possibly make me wait outside for the whole period. But then the bell rang and class ended, and the tiny sliver of hope that remained had disappeared.

After that depressing science period was reading, where we had a substitute teacher. Still distraught, I silently found a seat in the classroom and put my head down on the desk. Before the substitute had finished introducing himself, Mrs. Taylor stormed into the room and over to his desk.

"Excuse me, I'd like to make you aware of a situation, sir!" she barked. "Do you see that nasty child sitting over there?"

I picked up my head and saw that her hateful gaze and her crooked index finger were pointing at me.

"He's good for nothing creating disruptions!

Make sure he doesn't act up. And if he says anything stupid, go straight to the principal. Don't give him any warnings!"

"Understood. Thank you," muttered the substitute. His eyes had turned cold.

I was speechless as Mrs. Taylor stormed out of the room. She had to pass me as she walked out the door, and I noticed that she was gritting her teeth in hatred. I was mortified.

Mrs. Taylor spoiled my relationships with several other teachers, some of whom I'd never even had class with before. Word spread among the teachers that I was the most outrageous student in the lower school. Many teachers I'd previously gotten along with seemingly turned their backs on me. Our art teacher, Mrs. Katz, who happened to be good friends with Mrs. Taylor stopped talking to me altogether. She no longer responded when I greeted her in the hallways, she ignored me when I raised my hand in her class, and she always came to me last when she was handing out art supplies, which often meant that I got the broken pencils or crayons that nobody else wanted.

My homeroom teacher, Mr. Poolen, wasn't much better. One day during recess, when I ran back to homeroom to get a football from my backpack, I saw Mrs. Taylor and Mr. Poolen talking at his desk.

"Hi, Mrs. Taylor," I said politely.

"What is it?" she snapped.

I expected nothing less than rudeness from her at that point, but I didn't respond in kind. "Nothing, ma'am. I was just saying hi."

"Excuse me! Don't you see we're having a discussion!" thundered Mr. Poolen.

His anger startled me. He'd never yelled at me before, and I couldn't figure out what I'd done wrong to him. But I knew better than to stick around, so I quickly left the classroom with my football in my hand and a lump in my throat. From that day forward, Mr. Poolen made sure I knew he disliked me.

About a month later, Grandma Lucy's second husband died. That week, Aunt Candace came down from Pennsylvania to host a celebration of his life at Grandma's house. The party was rather large, and it included catering, a gift exchange, speeches, and a special ceremony. Everybody was going to attend because the event offered closure for the life of a highly distinguished major in the Marines. Aunt Candace, however, made sure that I was excluded from the festivities by mandating that no children were allowed, but I didn't find out until the night of the party, when Mommy and Daddy called the babysitter to our house.

That night I cried. And cried. And cried. My tears were bitter, and my eyes stung. *Why does Aunt Candace hate me so much? I've grown up! It wasn't like I was gonna bother her by asking to play board games or football with her!*

Micah and I were the only children in the family, and the bottom line was that we were unwanted. To our white family members, we were walking reminders that my mother had married a Black man, and they detested it.

But the death of Grandma Lucy's husband did change that dynamic somewhat. Grandma was now alone in her large home, and she started longing for company. She turned her attention to me for the first time in my life. She invited me to spend the night at her house regularly, which was thrilling because I was never invited anywhere. It was slightly confusing that Grandma never invited Micah to come along, but I guessed that she thought that he was too

29

young, and maybe Grandma Lucy had never before taken care of small children alone.

Grandma and I ate dinner, then we played solitaire at her kitchen table for hours, using her favorite two decks of cards. We joked together the entire time, and with her nimble fingers, she often beat me and threw her hands up in celebration as we both screamed with laughter. Then we retired to her room, where we watched television until one of us was too tired to keep our eyes open. I gave Grandma a kiss and walked across the hall to the bedroom I stayed in. That room was amazing. It had its own cable television, something I wasn't accustomed to having in my bedroom. Every aspect of staying at Grandma's house was special to me and helped me forget that I didn't have any friends.

Usually when I stayed at her house, on the second day of my stay, Grandma Lucy would take me to the skatepark ten minutes from her home. I spent hours there, and eventually I learned how to drop in and carve my way about the half-pipe. I was usually the youngest skateboarder by far, but the skills I'd learned allowed me to integrate properly with other skaters and bikers. The kids I met there began teaching me new things, and within a few months, I'd transitioned from watching Tim back at home to skating with him. He no longer gave me the cold shoulder when I rode down the street to meet him. We were far from being friends, but at least he tolerated me.

Not long after I developed a relationship with Grandma Lucy, I found out about the birth of my first cousin, Aunt Candace's daughter. I was so excited finally to be a big cousin! I hoped Aunt Candace would bring her to our house. But she lived in Pennsylvania, and something in the pit of my stomach told me that we wouldn't be seeing her anytime soon. The brightness of my excitement soon dimmed, though, when I learned that Aunt Candace had named her baby Sarah, which was the name of my older sister, who had died at birth. That seemed spiteful, even to me.

"Mommy, why did Aunt Candace pick the same name as my dead sister," I asked one day.

"Don't worry, sweetheart. It's just a coincidence."

Mom always had such an amazingly graceful nature that even in light of something this painful, she maintained her composure and managed to soothe me.

Of all the names in the world, why that one? It seemed calculated to hurt our feelings. I could only imagine how Mommy must have felt. It wasn't like Aunt Candace had consulted Mommy first to ask how she felt about naming her daughter in *honor* of my big sister. It was yet another blatant slap in the face to our mixed-race family.

My homeroom teacher, Mr. Poolen, started treating me like a dog, but I continued to excel academically in all of my third grade classes. Even Mrs. Taylor's campaign against me didn't affect my overall mood. In fact, my morale was relatively high that year.

That all changed one day in PE, however. We were playing lacrosse, and I'd won three face-offs in a row, and I'd scored the first two goals of the game. The fourth face-off was against a classmate named Dave. I won the ball effortlessly and dashed for our opponent's goal. Dancing around the box, I disoriented the goalie before skillfully slinging the ball behind my back for an outstanding goal. My team was ecstatic.

Dave, whom I'd left trailing behind me, stormed up to me, enraged, and screamed in my face, "Stop showing off, you idiot!"

"Whoa, dude," I responded calmly. "It's just a game, man. There's no need to get worked up. We're all friends."

The entire class had stopped playing to listen to our argument.

"Actually, that's false, buddy boy," Dave snapped. "How many birthday parties do you get invited to? I'm pretty sure I've never seen you at anybody's party in the whole school. Except Kevin, and you just got invited to his party because he's a weird Indian."

My heart stopped. "What are you talking about? I go to parties," I retorted. But Dave *did* have a point, and I was suddenly more embarrassed than I'd ever been in my life.

"And, by the way, what are you anyway? Black?" he continued.

"No, I'm regular. Just like you," I answered.

"But I thought your dad was from Nigeria. And just look at your hair. Doesn't that make you Black?"

I didn't know what to say to that. I wondered if I should own the fact that my hair was different.

"And if you're Black, then why don't you talk Black? Why do you sound so white?" Dave needled.

I just shrugged. Everybody watched and listened in silence. I wanted to disappear.

"Let's take a poll," he suggested. "Whoever is Drew's friend, raise their hand."

Nobody moved. Kids who were cordial and kids I routinely joked with were silent. Not a single hand was raised.

"Nate, you said we were friends yesterday," I mumbled to the teammate who was standing next to me.

From the look in Nate's eyes, I could see he was too afraid to do anything that would alienate him among the popular kids. My head drooped. I wished I could press a button and fast forward time. Even if everybody came back to school the next day and decided to play with me at recess, nobody was going to forget that confrontation.

As Dave's popularity grew, my popularity waned. By the fourth grade, I didn't have the right to laugh when my classmates laughed. If someone told a joke and I laughed, someone would say, "Drew, what's so funny? Nobody was talking to you."

Dave regularly took class polls. "Everybody here—who likes Drew? Raise your hand."

I remember the icy feeling that ran through my veins each time. Not a single soul was brave enough to come to my defense. But could you blame them? You can't just put fourth graders on the spot and expect them to stand up for the most unpopular kid in the school.

Things got even worse when Dave joined the recreational lacrosse league I'd been playing in for about two years. My league was made up almost entirely of white private school boys from exceedingly affluent families, and until that day, we got along well. I was the star of my team, and the coach always used me as an example when demonstrating drills for the rest of the team, but when Dave joined, he made it his mission to destroy me.

On his first day on the team, Dave screamed, "Ball hog!" after I scored the first goal of our scrimmage.

My teammates looked at him, and then at me, as if

trying to make their minds up about whether he was right. I ignored him.

When everybody had congregated on the sidelines during half time, Dave took a particularly malicious shot at me. "Hey, Drew. Can you do this?" Dave removed his helmet and shook his long blonde hair from side to side. "Normal people can shake out their hair."

The entire team stared at me, and I could feel their eyes studying my nappy hair, which undoubtedly carried the unsightly imprint of my lacrosse helmet. My cheeks burned in embarrassment, but I fought to stay calm. "Dude, why are you trying to start trouble? Can't we just be friends?"

Dave laughed loudly, then said, "What are you talking about, man? You have zero friends. Don't try and act like everybody at school doesn't hate you."

I couldn't believe my ears. My only place of solace was about to turn into yet another source of pain. I wanted badly to hit Dave, but I knew that wasn't an option. My parents had taught me my entire life that they wouldn't tolerate any physical altercations, and fighting at King's Hall was forbidden, even if it was in self-defense. Students were instructed to inform a teacher if somebody was harassing them, but they weren't ever permitted to strike anybody. That would be grounds for immediate suspension.

But none of that stopped me from using my words to fight back. "Get out of my freaking face, you idiot!" I shouted at Dave. "Nobody's listening to you!" I knew that wasn't true, but it was my best defense at that point.

By the end of practice, Dave had already made two new friends. I began feeling that things on the team were never going to be the same again.

Within three weeks, my rec league teammates had stopped passing me the ball during practices. It got so bad that when our team had games against other teams, my teammates wouldn't pass me the ball, even if I was the only man open. That lead to frequent turnovers. Perhaps the most alarming realization was that my coach turned a blind eye to what was happening because his son, who was on the team, had recently become a good friend of Dave's.

That Christmas, something interesting happened. As we sat around our Christmas tree opening gifts, Mommy began reading a card from Aunt Candace. She described her new ultra-expensive and exotic sedan, which Greg had given her as an early present. She went into great detail about the various luxury features. As Mommy read, I remember feeling so happy and excited for my aunt. I'd never been inside such a car, and I was intrigued by everything she described.

"Mommy, how expensive was the car?" I asked.

"Oh, honey. I'm not sure, but it certainly is one of a kind," she explained with a warm smile on her face.

Aunt Candace went on to say that one of her friends at their exclusive country club had persuaded her to purchase a $15,000 watch for Greg.

As I listened to her letter, I couldn't help feeling eager to open the gifts that Aunt Candace and Uncle Greg had sent us. They were the last ones under the tree, and I guessed that they would be the best of the bunch.

As I unwrapped my gift, I couldn't contain my excitement. But when I ripped the box open, my face twisted in confusion. She'd given us a stack of used computer games, crudely bound by several crusty rubber bands. They were the games that Greg had discarded from his home office.

"Wow, this is cool!" I exclaimed, trying to sound

enthused. It wasn't that I was unhappy or ungrateful. I just couldn't help but notice that many of the disks were scratched, and they weren't even in their original jewel cases. They were also so old that the front of the CDs had begun to fade. Mommy, Daddy, and Micah's gifts from Aunt Candace and Uncle Greg were equally horrendous.

I went down to the basement to try out a few of the games. Fewer than half of them even worked. I just couldn't comprehend the meanness.

In the new year, I began to skateboard much more often. I learned to kick-flip and grind on objects as high as a park bench. And I was known as the best skateboarder in the entire school, which amazed my classmates just as much as it enraged them. On days when the lower school got out early to watch the upper school varsity football games, I rode my skateboard through campus, dazzling my peers and the upperclassmen with various combinations of tricks. Whenever I landed a trick, people yelled and cheered me on. I momentarily felt like I was in a different world—a perfect world.

There was a particular staircase at the bottom of one of the hills leading down to the gym, and the day I successfully jumped it for the first time was the day I earned the nickname "The Skater" at King's Hall. I jumped the set of five stairs over and over until I was comfortable enough to land a 180 spin. Eventually a crowd of kids gathered around the staircase, and each time I attempted it, they hollered at the top of their lungs. The adrenaline pumping in my veins numbed my body so that even when I fell, I immediately sprang up and tried again.

The one problem with my new nickname and my

budding reputation was that my newfound popularity also created a great deal of envy among the most popular of my classmates, particularly a boy named Christopher. He was regarded as the skateboard guru, and his divorced mother had bought him more than thirty-five different high-line skateboards. Each one cost around $175, so anytime skateboarding came up in school, everyone listened to him. Never before had he and I clashed, but the week after my staircase jump, one of our classmates brought up skating, and Christopher showed his true colors.

We were taking a short break from handwriting lessons when Jeff, a levelheaded boy, said, "Dude, did you guys see Drew skateboarding the other day? He jumped the entire staircase at the bottom of the hill, and now all the tenth graders are calling him The Skater!"

Pride welling up inside, I glanced over at Jeff.

"Oh my gosh! Who cares?!" Christopher spat.

I looked over at Christopher in horror. His face was red, and his brow was knit.

"Hey, Drew. How 'bout you stop being a stupid showoff and get some friends!" said Christopher.

"Ha!" Dave yelled from across the room. "You see what I've been saying, dude. Everyone hates you, Drew, you frizzy-headed freak."

I glanced over at the teacher, who was pretending to bury his face in a newspaper. It was obvious he had no intention of intervening. I became irate. *This is so racist!* I thought. Well if the teacher wasn't going to say anything, I would.

"Just because you guys suck at everything you do doesn't mean you have to take your frustration out on me. Grow up!" I retorted.

Our handwriting teacher immediately rose to his feet.

"Excuse me, Drew! Who do you think you are, talking to people like that?" he scolded. "Go to the principal's office now!"

That old familiar feeling that the entire universe was against me returned. No matter how one-sided things were, the faculty didn't seem to care. I came to the realization that teachers in the school were either too afraid to vex the sons of the wealthy King's Hall donors, or they simply hated me for who I was.

I marched out of the classroom and to the principal's office. I was enraged by the injustice of it all, but the principal didn't want to hear my explanation. He called my parents for the umpteenth time to tell them that I was "disturbing class once again."

In the fifth grade, the only times I didn't wear a hat or hoodie was when I was in the classroom. I figured that if my hair was covered and people only saw my white skin, people would accept me. When the hat was on, I felt like a human being. I'd become deeply afraid of being in public because I thought everyone saw me as a weird, ugly loner. I was extremely sensitive about my hair because, in my mind, it was abnormal. I felt like I had a disgusting, spongy parasite permanently latched onto my head, dooming me to eternal friendlessness.

Whenever I needed to comb my hair, I hid. My new name at school was "Oreo," a word that weakened my will to exist. The teachers at my all-white school continued to turn a blind eye to the bullying that was eating at my soul. They increasingly saw me as the "troubled" child, and rather than helping me, they seemed to have joined forces with the mean kids. I

One episode in fifth grade was especially disheartening. It involved Mr. Dillon, whose duty it was to oversee our PE class. We played baseball that day, and before our game started, Mr. Dillon lead us through a warmup exercise.

"All right, boys. Break into pairs so you can practice your throws and catches."

Butterflies immediately fluttered in the pit of my stomach, which happened every time we were told to break into pairs because I knew that I was going to be the odd man out. Sure enough, the entire class quickly found their partners, and I was left alone. Not seeing any alternative, I approached Mr. Dillon and discretely asked if he wouldn't mind being my partner.

"Oh wow, buddy. Isn't that what your friends are for?" Mr. Dillon responded in a loud voice, intentionally bringing attention to our conversation.

Many children in the class giggled from across the field as they threw baseballs back and forth.

"I'm sorry, I just don't have a partner to catch with," I explained.

Mr. Dillon suddenly exploded. "Sorry, sorry, sorry! That's all you know how to say! Jeez, you sure are a sorry fellow, aren't you?"

Eyes wide, I froze. I was completely humiliated, and several kids were laughing heartily at me.

"Did you hear that, sponge-head? Everybody hates you! Even the teacher!" Dave screamed from across the field.

I looked at Mr. Dillon, hoping that he'd either come to my defense or reprimand Dave, but he did nothing of the sort. Instead, Mr. Dillon stormed over to his gym bag, angrily pulled out a glove, and reluctantly played catch with me.

Before the first quarter of my fifth grade school year had ended, my parents decided to pull me out of King's Hall. The psychological trauma that I endured every day was wearing on me emotionally. Gone was the pride I'd felt at calling myself a King's Hall student. The beautiful campus, sports facilities, and state-of-the-art classrooms—all gone. I could no longer wear the dark blue shirts and sweaters bearing the royal King's Hall crest. I felt like my life had ended.

4

STOP TRYING TO BE COOL

Before the end of fifth grade, we moved into a suburban neighborhood. I'd been whisked away from the prestigious King's Hall school, and I found myself in a local public school. The world I knew had come crashing down around me. King's Hall had sports teams, lacrosse fields, football fields, tennis courts, multiple recreational centers, various cafeterias, a large school store, and all the reputation you could possibly ask for. My new elementary school had a gym the size of a swimming pool...and that was about it. That made me downright depressed.

In Maryland, going to a private school was a thing to brag about. In fact, most parents are nearly as proud of having a child in private school as they are of having one at an Ivy League university. The children in my new elementary school didn't seem to have anything against me, but I was scared to reach out and make friends. Half the time, I expected someone to yell, "You have no friends! Stop trying to be cool!" I went through the remainder of the school year in a zombie-like state of self-pity.

· · ·

That December, Aunt Candace called our house and instructed my brother and me to each write a list of five things we wanted for Christmas. She told us that she would get us each two things from the lists and that there was no price restriction. What?!

As soon as we got off the phone, my brother and I excitedly began writing. I wrote that I wanted a handheld gaming system, skateboard shoes, a new lacrosse stick, a yo-yo, and binoculars. Micah wanted a dart gun, a scooter, playing cards, a digital watch, and a military flashlight. Even though our aunt had specified there wasn't a price limit, we knew not to ask for anything too expensive. That would be impolite.

We mailed our lists to her that same day. When it came time to open Aunt Candace's gift on the 25th, I could see by the size of my box that it couldn't be anything other than a handheld gaming system. Excitement pulsed through my body. I'd totally forgotten about the previous year's debacle. It was so wonderful to have an Aunt who would buy me the gift that I wanted more than anything else, the first gift on my list. Grinning broadly, I tore through the wrapping paper and discovered...a box of crayons.

Was this a prank? I searched for my second gift, but there was nothing else under the tree. I looked over at my brother, who had unwrapped the exact same gift. He started crying.

"Mommy, why did Aunt Candace tell us to write lists if she didn't actually plan on getting us anything we wanted?" I asked.

"Now, dear, be grateful," Mommy responded.

The worst part of it was that Mommy told us that we had to write thank-you cards to our aunt. We obeyed, but only reluctantly.

Before I knew it, I was a student at the local public middle school, along with more than 300 other sixth graders. Never before had I seen so many kids in one grade. Not more than a month after the beginning of middle school, Aunt Candace, Uncle Greg, and little Sarah came down from Pennsylvania to visit Grandma Lucy.

"Well, boys, you're finally going to get to see your little cousin," Mommy said.

"Yaaay!" my brother and I exclaimed in unison.

"I can't wait to see Sarah!" said Micah.

"I know. This is going to be great!" I added.

That Friday, during their week-long stay, we arranged a visit at Grandma's house around noon, and we pulled up to her house right on the dot. Before getting out of the car, I covered my head with my black beanie and rushed up Grandma's driveway, past Aunt Candace's super-expensive car.

I rang the doorbell. No reply. I waited for about forty-five seconds before ringing the doorbell again.

"Mommy, aren't they home?" I called back to my mother, who was making her way up the driveway with Daddy and Micah.

"Yes, honey. Just be patient," she replied.

I waited for another minute before turning to my parents, who were now standing next to me outside Grandma's front door.

"What's going on?" I asked Mommy.

At that very instant, the door swung open, and there stood Grandma Lucy.

"Hi, Grandma!" I exclaimed.

"Shh!" she snapped.

Her face was cold. Her expression spoke to her annoyance. I stood stunned.

"Your little cousin is asleep!" she barked.

Never before had Grandma spoken to me so harshly. As we filed into her house, I couldn't help but feel a little bit rejected. In her living room, not more than fifteen feet from the door, sat Aunt Candace and Uncle Greg, watching television. Neither one turned to acknowledge our presence until my mother greeted them.

I wondered why they'd left us standing outside for nearly two minutes after I'd rung the bell, but I quickly pushed the thought to the back of my mind. I walked up to my aunt and uncle and gave them both hugs. Micah did the same, then he sat next to me on the couch. Uncle Greg began to make small talk with us while Mommy and Daddy talked to Aunt Candace.

A few minutes later, Grandma entered the living room, holding Sarah's hand. My heart was filled with unadulterated joy. I walked over to my little cousin and picked her up.

"Hi there, Sarah, I'm your big cousin. My name's Drew," I said warmly.

Sarah's entire face lit up, and she said, "Hi, Drew."

She was the cutest little thing I'd ever seen, and I instantly fell in love with her. Aunt Candace and Uncle Greg fell silent, and they watched me intently.

"You have such beautiful blond hair, Sarah. Just like an angel," I said.

Sarah giggled and planted a big kiss on my nose.

All of a sudden, Aunt Candace sprang to her feet, charged me, and yelled, "No, Sarah!" She jerked the little girl from my arms and sternly reprimanded her. "You do *not* kiss them. Do you understand me?"

Sarah began to cry, and I was extremely uneasy. The

room was suddenly very tense. I honestly wasn't sure if Uncle Greg was going to rush toward me and punch me in the face. I sat back down on the couch next to my brother, and I glanced across the room at my parents in despair.

It was time for lunch, and all of us congregated in Grandma Lucy's dining room at the large, round table. Grandma instructed me to remove my hat. As Uncle Greg and Daddy talked, Mommy, Aunt Candace, and Grandma shared forced laughter.

"Hey, Drew, why don't you tell your aunt about your lacrosse skills?" said Mommy.

That sounded like a good idea, so I excitedly told Aunt Candace about how frequently I won face-offs and about how I was the fastest player on my team. I was in the middle of recounting the various time I'd won the game with a magnificent last-minute goal when Uncle Greg interrupted my story.

"Hey, buddy. Why don't you run down to the pond and feed the geese?" He shoved a plate of croutons in my direction.

I didn't initially perceive his suggestion as hostile, but I did know that the pond was more than a quarter of a mile from the house, and I wasn't finished eating lunch yet.

"Son, stay right where you are and enjoy your food," said Daddy, contradicting Uncle Greg's ridiculous suggestion.

My parent's gracious and forgiving nature consistently prevented awkward situations from devolving into full-blown arguments.

A few moments later, Aunt Candace asked Mommy, "So, are you coming to our party tomorrow?"

My ears perked up, and I looked over at my brother. He looked as excited as I felt.

"Oh, cool. We're having a party?" I blurted.

Aunt Candace wasn't looking at me when she responded coldly, "This is an adult party, Drew. Children aren't welcome."

I looked to my mother, my eyes full of hurt.

"We'll have to check our schedule, Candace," she replied.

I turned to Daddy to gauge his reaction. He was visibly upset. His slanted brows told of his frustration. We left as soon as we were finished with lunch.

The next evening, Mommy, Daddy, Micah, and I were playing a family board game in our living room when the telephone rang. Mommy answered it on speaker phone. Grandma Lucy's artificially cheerful voice was broadcasted across the room.

"Our party has started, dear," she said. "Are you and your husband still planning on coming over?"

"We're having family time over here tonight," Mommy replied.

In the background I heard the voices of several adults, but I also heard Sarah's little laugh through the phone. The four of us silently listened, and time seemed to stand still.

"All right, dear. Well if you change your mind, just get a babysitter for the boys and call me when you're on your way."

After Mommy hung up, I mumbled, "I thought no kids were allowed tonight."

"Don't worry, baby. We're going to have fun here, just the four of us," she replied, her voice soothing.

On the days I went to lacrosse practice, I wore my beanie onto the field, put my pads on, then quickly removed the hat and jammed my head into a lacrosse helmet. Not that it ever helped with the bullying. It seemed like the whole league was full of kids who refused to talk to me.

Bracing to quickly put my beanie on after removing my helmet

The days when my teammates respected me, back in lower school, were long gone. These days, my teammates got their kicks by mocking me, saying things like, "Didn't you get expelled from King's Hall?"

The first time I heard that particular insult was during a practice, right after I scored a goal. The defender I'd beaten to the goal angrily threw his helmet to the ground and snapped, "Dude, you think you're big and bad, don't you? Oh wait a minute, didn't you get kicked out of King's Hall, blackie?"

Humiliated doesn't do justice to how I felt. I told myself that nobody else had heard him, but the truth was that at least ten other kids had. "What are you talking about? I'm still in private school, and I'm white just like you. Look at my skin," I lied robotically.

He called my bluff. "Oh yeah? Where do you go to

school then, man? I bet you go to public school, just like all the other Blacks."

I couldn't contain my rage. "Get the heck out of my face!" I roared at the top of my lungs.

Our coach shouted for me to come over to the sideline, but it wasn't to congratulate me on the twenty-yard shot I'd ripped into the goal.

"Just what do you think you are doing talking to your teammate like that?" he scolded.

"Coach, that boy was making fun of me and being racist," I explained.

"How?"

I felt backed into a corner. I could either tell the coach not to worry about it—which would inevitably draw his ire —or I could confess that my teammate was accusing me of getting kicked out of school—which I didn't want anybody to overhear. Either way, I was going to lose.

Confrontations like that were happening more and more frequently, and it became obvious that the coaches cared more about staying in the good graces of my teammates than even acknowledging their bullying.

On the sideline after a reprimand from the coach

Feeling isolated and depressed on the sideline

In a lot of ways, life in public school was a lot better than life at King's Hall. I was getting exceptional grades, and I'd recently wowed the entire grade with a perfect piano performance during the school talent show. My saving grace was that no one at the school knew that I'd ever been a student at King's Hall.

That changed about mid-way through the year, when I recognized a boy at my school who was part of my lacrosse team. His name was Tommy. I'd never seen him at school before, and I prayed that he hadn't spotted me. But of course he had. He was one of the kids who thought it was funny to mock me about supposedly being kicked out of King's Hall.

I worried that he was going to start a rumor in my new school to alienate me, so the next day I approached him at lunch.

"Hey, man. Can I have a word with you?"

Tommy nodded and followed me out of the cafeteria. I explained to him that I hadn't been kicked out of school, that my parents had withdrawn me.

"Please don't ruin this school for me, man," I begged.

Tommy looked extremely disinterested. "Yeah, sheesh, whatever."

I extended my hand to him, and he reluctantly shook it before hurrying back to his lunch table.

A few weeks later, I was skateboarding around campus after school, dazzling my spectators. I loved hearing them say things like, "Whoa! Did you see that?" Those comments made the adrenaline course through my veins. I spotted a set of stairs and attempted to jump it. On my first run, I crashed hard, but I knew how to fall, and I was unhurt. On my second try, I nailed my landing. I practiced that set of stairs over and over until a huge group of kids who were waiting outside in the carpool line migrated over to watch me. It must have been at least twenty-five boys and girls. Then, out of nowhere, Tommy surfaced.

Hoping that our conversation had made an ally of him, I said, "Sup, man?"

He didn't respond.

I brushed it off and attempted the staircase again. This time I grabbed my board while soaring through the air for a perfect Indy. Flawless execution.

"This kid is nuts!" shouted an amazed eighth grader.

Walking back up the stairs, I saw Tommy glaring at me. His cold gaze peered through me.

"Drew, weren't you kicked out of King's Hall?" he asked in an obnoxiously loud voice. It was obvious that he wanted everyone in the crowd to hear him.

"What? Are you serious? He really got kicked out of that school?" said a random voice in the crowd.

"Yeah, duh. Everyone knows that," said Tommy. "Nobody liked him there because he was such a freaking showoff. Seems like he hasn't learned his lesson."

Tommy was full of spite, and over the next few weeks, he made sure to spread the word around the school that I'd been kicked out of King's Hall. My classmates began to approach me to find out if the rumors were true. Whenever I denied the accusations, I was met with skepticism.

"Well then why did you leave King's Hall and come to a public school?" they usually asked me.

It was extremely difficult for me to make new friends, and before the end of my first year of middle school, I was a loner once again.

———

When seventh grade rolled around, I made a promise to myself that I was going to be accepted into another private school. Getting into a private school was more work in middle school because candidates were no longer accepted solely on their parents' wealth. Academic merit was the biggest factor in their decision. I worked diligently day and night to maintain straight A's because I knew it would help me to distinguish myself among the pool of applicants.

At the same time, I desperately wanted friends. The

middle school that had once looked like such a promising place for me to make new friends had turned its back on me. The boys in my grade piggybacked on what Tommy had told them the previous year, and I got a reputation for being a showoff. I just couldn't find a group of friends I fit well with. I was just too different from everyone. I spoke too white to be accepted by the Black kids, and I looked too Black to be accepted by the white kids. I was somewhere in the middle, and nobody had the courage to reach out and accept me for who I was.

The children in our suburban neighborhood attended my middle school, and their cliques extended beyond the confines of the classroom. They rode their bikes past my house every day, and not once did they invite me out to play with them. It was more of the same painful exclusion I'd become accustomed to.

On Valentine's Day in seventh grade, I decided to try to talk with a girl name Leslie. She had silky, light-brown hair, beautiful hazel eyes, and cherry-red lips. And she played lacrosse too! Throughout sixth grade, she'd sat a few seats behind me in English class, but I was always too shy to approach her. I didn't think she'd like my kinky hair. But something inside me changed in seventh grade. For some reason, I thought I had a shot now.

I made a card using pink construction paper, and I cut out yellow and red hearts to decorate the front. I used one of my calligraphy pens to write a short, sweet poem about her beauty, and I signed it at the bottom with my name in a heart. I waited until lunch. Show time!

I approached Leslie at her lunch table, which was packed with many of the popular kids in the grade and several lacrosse players.

"Hey, Leslie. Happy Valentine's Day. I made you this card, and I really hope you like it."

Handing her the card, I saw several of the boys at the end of her table snickering. I decided that it would be best if I went back to my table to avoid putting any unnecessary pressure on her, so I walked away. I glanced back just in time to see her shoot up out of her seat and throw the beautifully constructed card, which I'd spent more than an hour working on, straight into the trashcan. *She didn't even read it,* I thought. I was totally embarrassed, and I resolved to never try anything like that again.

Later that day, one of the boys who'd been sitting next to Leslie at lunch started talking trash to me during algebra. My classmates were casually talking with one another when the boy asked, "What's up with the King's Hall wallet?"

"What do you mean, man?" I asked.

"What I mean, Oreo, is why in the world do you have a King's Hall wallet?" he snarled, pointing to the dark blue wallet sitting on my desk. "You go to a public school. Is that 'cause you were expelled?"

Everybody in class stopped talking and stared at me.

"Where is all of this animosity coming from," I shot back at him. "What did I ever do to you?"

"Oh shut up and get some friends, Velcro head!" he yelled.

"Shut your dirty mouth, scum!" I shouted.

"Drew, I won't tolerate insults in my class," reprimanded Mr. Morrison, our algebra teacher.

"Are you serious, sir? Didn't you hear anything he just said to me?" I said.

"Don't ask me if I'm serious. Who do you think you are?" scolded Mr. Morrison.

I pointed at the boy. "He just yelled Velcro head at me, and you didn't say a word until I responded to him!"

"I'm not going to sit here and argue with a little boy," said Mr. Morrison. "If you have a problem with the way I conduct my class, you'd better step out."

After Mr. Morrison sided with the racist boy, I started wearing my beanie more often. I genuinely believed that I was ugly. None of the girls in school talked to me, nobody wanted a white boy with nappy African hair as a friend, and even members of my own family rejected me. Mommy and Daddy told me that I was "one of the most handsome children on Earth," but all the evidence said otherwise. I didn't believe them one bit because they were my parents, and that's what parents are supposed to say.

On the nights after lacrosse practice, I usually cried. My parents did their best to console me, but my cheeks were wet as I fell asleep most nights. I also began punching large dents in the walls of my room. When I looked at my bloodied fists and the damaged walls, I was filled with self-hatred. Mommy and Daddy didn't deserve this.

Sleepovers at Grandma Lucy's house were my only non-toxic form of recreation outside of my home. She was a totally different person when Aunt Candace and her husband weren't around. I was grateful that she still offered to play solitaire and watch movies with me when we were alone. She was the closest thing I had to a best friend—but she was also a friend I couldn't fully trust.

Mommy visited Grandma's house every Wednesday. She spent hours with her, cleaning, picking up groceries, and simply showering her with love. She was an incredibly dedicated daughter. Once or twice a month, Mommy brought

Grandma over to our house to spend the night with us, and it was always very special. Grandma Lucy seemed to be the happiest person in the world when she visited, but it turned that was an illusion.

One day, Aunt Candace told the family that she'd received an executive position in her company and that she'd be moving to Texas. We were very happy for her, but shortly after Candace's announcement, Grandma called my mother and told her that she was going to be "leaving with her daughter." Mommy was distraught, and so were we.

Over the next few weeks, Grandma promised Mommy that she'd give her all the expensive furniture in her house because it wouldn't fit in her Texas apartment. The furniture was worth several tens of thousands of dollars, and even if we couldn't fit all of it in our house, we could sell it and use that money to pay off various loans.

Right before Grandma Lucy left, however, she pulled the rug from under us. She told Mommy that she was giving all of her furniture to wealthy Aunt Candace. Once again, Mommy had been slapped in the face.

Mommy wasn't the only person shaken up by the ordeal. Grandma was my only outlet outside of home for de-stressing, and she was disappearing. Visits to Grandma's house were about to be a thing of the past. *Doesn't she care about us? Didn't I tell her that she was my only friend?*

I felt betrayed, and I came to the realization that she'd had to choose between her white family and her Black family. She chose them because they weren't tainted.

5

HOW 'BOUT WE CALL YOU ZEBRA?

When I was accepted into the St. Mathicus community, I felt like my future had opened back up. The school was three times the size of King's Hall, had better sports teams, boasted modern buildings, and was far more prestigious. My excitement was indescribable. I was more than happy to dedicate the entire summer preparing for the topics that would be covered in the first month of classes. I was determined to be prepared when school started.

Eighth grade year, I carpooled every morning with a boy named Gerald and his older brother, Vlad. Gerald's mother had met my mother at a social gathering, and when they found out that he and I would soon be at the same school, they exchanged telephone numbers. Vlad had a muscle car that his parents purchased for him in a moment of bad judgment, not knowing that Vlad drove like a maniac every second he was behind the wheel. And I mean every second. On several occasions during the drive to school, we had near misses with vehicles on the opposite side of the road because Vlad constantly put his car sideways around the corners of twisting backroads. After dropping us off at the middle school, Vlad screeched away to the upper school, half a mile across campus.

Gerald and I walked into school together, and for the first time possibly ever, I knew the comforting feeling of having a friend who didn't mind standing next to me in front of others. I felt like a human being. That first week, I learned that there were no Black children in my grade, but that didn't trouble me because, in my denial, I considered myself white.

Gerald and I had completely different personalities. I loved to play sports, while he preferred to play card games in which participants dueled mythical creatures. I liked to talk about skateboarding, while he preferred to discuss his recent level advances as a top wizard in his favorite medieval-themed video games. I decided to find common ground with Gerald in the hope that our friendship would prove useful to my survival in the new school. I purchased a set of mythical creature cards, and I joined the group of friends that Gerald met nearly every day after school in the science lab to learn the game.

As I followed Gerald into the lab, I saw three kids from our class, who were extremely unkempt. Two of them looked dejected, and the third appeared cross-eyed and mildly autistic. None of that bothered me though. I introduced myself enthusiastically, which seemed to catch them off guard. I pulled out my cards to start the game when out of nowhere, the cross-eyed kid began venting about how much he hated everyone in our grade. He particularly hated the athletes. I couldn't pinpoint any specific reason why, but who was I to judge? I knew nothing about his history at the school. I kept quiet, listened, and waited for him to cool down.

When the game started, I realized within a few moments

that I had absolutely no interest in it. I tried to pretend that rolling the twenty-sided die to battle elves, wizards, and goblins was fascinating, but it was all a front. I was desperate for friends who wouldn't jeer at me. And if I had friends, no one could ridicule me for not having any. I could breathe easy.

The next week we had our first gym class of the year. The gym instructor threw us a football and told us to divide into teams. The familiar feeling of panic shot through my body, and butterflies danced in the pit of my stomach. I was afraid that they would reject me the same way they had at King's Hall. But to my relief, one of the team captains chose me as his third teammate. I was elated, but I tried not to let it show.

We began to play a few minutes later. As I rocketed down the field, our quarterback saw the space I'd created and tossed the ball in my direction. I caught it with one hand and effortlessly galloped into the end zone. Not a bad way to start a game! My teammates raced over to me to celebrate the first touchdown of the game, and the players on the other team gave us the stink eye.

After I scored two more touchdowns, a kid on the opposing team began hurling profanities. Some of the kids on my team weren't as ecstatic anymore either. I realized that my classmates, many of whom had known each other for years, didn't seem thrilled to learn that the new kid was also a gifted athlete. I didn't play nearly as hard for the rest of the game because I wanted to avoid creating a rift between my classmates and me.

The next period, our teacher left the room briefly to run down to the main office for supplies. The kid who'd been cursing during the game, whose name was Andy, took the opportunity to go on the offensive.

"Hey, pal," he called from across the room in a Southern accent. "Where you from?"

"Central Maryland. How 'bout you, bro?"

"No, I mean where did you originate? Like where is your Daddy from?" he clarified.

The traumas of earlier racially charged confrontations made my tone harsh. "My father's from Nigeria."

Half of the class turned around in their seats to look at me, and I could feel their eyes poking my nappy hair.

"You guys are good runners, aren't you?" Andy continued.

"Everybody can run. It really doesn't matter what country you come from," I reasoned. I could feel his hatred beginning to sprout.

"You're a light one, aren't you? How 'bout we call you zebra?" he suggested, grinning maliciously.

Unbelievable. He was jabbing me with racial slurs just because I scored a couple touchdowns in a meaningless game.

"I'd prefer you didn't call me that," I responded.

One or two of his friends snickered quietly around him. They'd been on the opposing team in gym class too.

The teacher returned just then, and he continued his lesson. As much as I wanted to pretend that the confrontation with Andy didn't mean anything, I could sense that the classroom dynamic had shifted radically in those moments.

Unable to escape to Grandma Lucy's house, I felt increasingly isolated. Mommy and Daddy must have recognized my low spirits because they suggested that I join Maximize, the youth group at our local church. I agreed to give it a try, hoping that something good would come from branching out. Every Friday night, I donned my beanie and left for Maximize, where I eventually joined the drama team. The team put together various videos, and we had to practice over and over again until we had perfected our act. On occasion, we performed in front of the entire church congregation on Sundays.

Things were going fine until one Friday evening, when the twenty-one-year-old sister of our team leader made a snide comment about my Princeton T-shirt.

"Hey, Drew. Why do you always wear Princeton stuff? Do you *go* to Princeton?" she snarked.

"No, I'm only in eighth grade. But I want to go there someday." I tried to keep my voice mellow.

"You mean for school? Yeah, no way you're getting into Princeton," she scoffed.

"Why do you say that?" I asked.

"Because nobody gets into Princeton. Trust me, I tried!" she snapped in a raised voice.

I came to find out that she attended a local community college, and she grew increasingly bitter toward me because of my Ivy League ambitions. From the night she confronted me over my shirt, she seemed to have nothing but disdain for me.

Things got really scary in Maximize really quickly. The videos that our group produced took an extremely dark turn. One day our drama team leader decided to re-enact a KKK lynching of a Black worshipper, and he chose me to be the victim. I was the only member of the group who wasn't completely white, and I guess in his mind it only made sense to cast me as the victim. I wondered what made it so obvious to them. I always wore my beanie at Maximize, so it was almost impossible to see my kinky hair. For a fleeting moment, I wondered if the twenty-one-year-old sister of our team leader had orchestrated my role in that horrific skit.

I hated that they wanted me to portray the Black character. That was literally the last thing I wanted to do. But I obliged our team leader and played the part, trying with all my might not to let my insecurity show. That was one of the hardest things I've ever done.

A couple months later, I joined the St. Mathicus eighth grade soccer team, and I quickly became their best player. I was careful to display great humility because my athleticism had previously drawn so much negativity from jealous peers. I wasn't going to let that do me in this time.

Around that time, I found out that Andy's father basically owned half of St. Mathicus. He'd made significant financial contributions to the construction of several state-of-the-art facilities across campus, and his family name was engraved on a plaque in front of one of the school gyms that he'd built. I wished it had been anyone else's son who had hurled racial slurs at me, someone with less influence. I was all too familiar with the fact that rich kids had teachers wrapped around their fingers. If things kept going downhill with Andy, there would likely be no turning back.

I decided to try a different tack this time. I devised a plan of action with one goal: to get Andy to like me. Before I could put my plan into effect though, Andy caught me off guard one day after school.

I'd just walked into the science wing with Gerald and his three friends so we could play another dreadful game. We hadn't been seated for more than two minutes when Andy walked in.

"Looks like you nerds found yourself a new friend!" he

said to Gerald. "You wouldn't have known he was a card freak like y'all judging from the way he plays football." Looking at me, he added, "Ain't that right, zebra?"

I couldn't hold my tongue. "Hey, man. Quit being racist. I told you not to call me that. What's your problem?" I barked back at him.

I glanced over at Gerald's cross-eyed friend, who was now staring at me in disgust. Andy had just blown my cover! I figured that the cross-eyed kid was likely going to hate me just as much as he hated all the other athletes in our school.

"You sure do have a mouth on you, boy," Andy jeered as he walked away.

I turned back to Gerald's group, hoping that we'd be able to resume our game in peace, but the cross-eyed kid suddenly rose to his feet and angrily flipped over our game table. I looked him in the eyes and for a fleeting moment and saw the face of a psychopathic school shooter. He threw his belongings into a backpack and stormed out.

The rest of us sat in awkward silence.

"Sooo," Gerald said. "What in the world did you do to piss off Andy, Drew?"

"Nothing," I replied. "The guy has been treating me like crap from day one, man."

"He's definitely not the one you want mad at you," said Gerald.

Great. Just Great.

During PE class a couple weeks later, we played dodgeball. The teacher had us divide ourselves just as we had when we played football. Andy was one of the team captains, and he picked all his friends. Lo and behold, I ended up on the opposing team again. The gym teacher lined all the balls up in the middle of the court and blew the whistle. Then everyone either rushed to grab one or ran for cover.

I was one of the first to midcourt, and I held a dodgeball in my hand to deflect any balls thrown at me. I didn't want to start pegging kids immediately at my new school.

Andy started counting down: "Three, two, one—" He and four of his teammates launched their balls at me all at once. I dodged three that were aimed at my face, deflecting the fourth and effectively thwarting their coordinated attack. If he wanted to play dirty...I beamed a ball across the court at one of the boys who had attacked me. It smashed into his chest so hard that he was unable to catch it.

"Ohhhh!" some of my teammates shouted at the thump of the impact.

The boy reluctantly slithered off to the sideline. Andy and two of his teammates once again threw their dodgeballs at me in unison, but I was too quick for them. My counterattack was vicious. I launched my ball directly at Andy, smashing him in the side of his neck as he attempted to duck. Perfect execution.

Andy began screaming at me, "So it's like that, zebra? Well screw you then. You'll see!"

"Great sportsmanship," I retorted, ignoring his racist rant. I'd resolved to face Andy like a man because clearly there was no alternative.

That day after school, I walked into the science wing, hoping to find Gerald and his friends in good spirits. Instead, I was met with hostility. The cross-eyed boy wanted nothing to do with me, and Gerald wasn't about to undermine the relationship he had with his friend of ten years. I left with a feeling of despair sitting heavy in my stomach.

The days and weeks that followed proved to be very awkward between Gerald and me. His brother arrived at our house in the morning, and Gerald silently got out of the coupe and moved his seat up for me to climb in the backseat behind him. He didn't say a single, solitary word to me, even though I always said good morning to him. Vlad responded, but the most I could ever get out of Gerald was a mumble or a grunt. Once again, I'd successfully become the most unpopular kid in my grade.

Lunchtime was one of the most traumatic periods of the day. As soon as I set my lunchbox down at a table, the students at whichever table I chose all got up in unison and relocated. The most humiliating part was that sixth and seventh graders laughed at me at the top of their lungs. My heart could barely handle the isolation and the taunting that I braved as I sat by myself day after day.

Our annual middle school camping trip was during the second quarter of the school year. The day before we left, our teachers had all the eighth grade homerooms congregate in the English wing to discuss our itinerary. During that meeting, I made one of the biggest blunders of my scholastic career.

Near the end of our meeting, I realized that nobody had mentioned rules regarding electronics. Having never attended one of the St. Mathicus camping trips, I innocently raised my hand and asked, "Can we bring electronic devices?"

A teacher who had a reputation for being mean to the not-so-popular kids said, "Oh, yeah. Thank you for reminding me, Drew. Absolutely no electronics!" He had a wicked smirk on his face.

I realized my mistake as my classmates mumbled invectives.

"Great going, idiot!"

"Oh my God. What the hell?!"

"Freaking bigmouth!"

The trip was pure misery. I was totally isolated the whole time. My classmates either ignored me or subjected me to cruel jokes and criticism. There's nothing worse than knowing that you're the most hated person in a group that you're forced to be a part of, especially when all you want to do is make new friends.

I finished the rest of the school year as a loner. My only hope was that the new students who would join us next year for the start of high school would be more open to friendship. If they didn't know the history of my unpopularity, I might have a chance.

That Christmas, Aunt Candace struck again. But this time, my brother and I were fully aware of her contempt for us. As we sat around the tree, Mommy opened an envelope from Aunt Candace and Uncle Greg. Inside it were ten to fifteen pictures of a *new* mansion in Austin, which they'd purchased three months ago. The photos were in a customized card with a cover of their family posing in front of the house. Awestruck, Micah and I marveled at the photographs. They had a massive swimming pool, twenty-foot ceilings, a cutting-edge kitchen full of stainless steel appliances, king-size beds in each of the six bedrooms, a movie theatre, a five-car garage, and many other extravagant amenities. The intricacy of the architecture was something that we'd never seen before.

My respect for my aunt skyrocketed. At that moment, I resolved to be just as wealthy as she and Uncle Greg. If I had a house like that, my parents and brother would be able to live with me whenever they wanted, and I'd have an amazing venue for hosting family parties. Most importantly, I wanted to make my parents proud.

Our gifts that year were just as atrocious as the years before. She seemed to revel in punishing her half-Black nephews. Micah and I unwrapped our gifts at the same time. He got a generic deodorant set from the dollar store. I got a bottle of shampoo. Yep, she gave us toiletries.

My mother got an eleven-by-eleven wooden plaque with a musical note printed in the middle of it.

"What does that mean?" I asked Mommy.

"Honey, let's please not make this an unpleasant Christmas," she responded, her tone exasperated.

I watched my father unwrap a pair of plain black dress socks.

"Mommy, I'm not trying to ruin the vibe right now," I said, "but I can't help but notice that she went on a dollar store shopping spree. We don't even do that to our neighbors."

"I need you to cut it out. Now," she demanded.

I looked to Micah for moral support. His face reflected my heartbreak. I knew that Christmas wasn't about the gifts, but I just couldn't understand why Aunt Candace chose to flaunt an affluent lifestyle in our faces through pictures and give us donation-level gifts.

In ninth grade, Vlad and Gerald stopped giving me rides. I began to worry that my high school experience would be a repeat of my years in middle school. But I shook off that fear and resolved to walk a different path. I'd reach out to kids who had no idea who I was.

My first interaction with the new students was during junior varsity lacrosse tryouts. Within the first week of school, I'd formed a ring of friends made entirely of the new kids who only knew me as a talented lacrosse player.

Of all the new guys, Jim, who'd moved from Virginia to join our school, was the one I got along with best. He was the midfielder I always flicked the ball to after I won the face-off. We sat next to each other in English class, exchanging jokes, and we ate lunch together in the cafeteria every day. After we finished eating, we took out our lacrosse sticks and threw balls back and forth. Since the cafeteria was the only place the boys had a chance to interact with the St. Mathicus girls' school, we felt great pride in showing off our lacrosse skills in front of them. The other new kids from our grade soon began bringing their lacrosse sticks to lunch to join us. I felt like a popular kid, but I couldn't help noticing Andy and his friends glaring at us through the cafeteria windows.

For the first time in my life, rather than walking into school in the morning with butterflies in my stomach, dreading what I might face that day, I was excited and energized. The relationships I formed with the new kids during tryouts lasted well into the second month of school. By that time, they were sitting with me in the cafeteria during lunch, completely unaware that I was considered uncool to the other kids in the grade. Girls even started joining us at our table, which was a totally new experience for us. Not that any of the boys could muster the courage to talk with them.

Ninth grade yearbook photo

Everything was going perfectly until Andy began paying special attention to Jim. Then one day it was as if somebody flipped a switch in Jim's head. He declined to play lacrosse at lunch, and he started sitting two chairs away from me in English. By the end of that month, Jim started dissing me for the first time.

Standing in front of Andy and his friends at lunch, Jim said, "I heard zebras can't make up their minds. Black or white?"

"What are you talking about, dude?" I responded.

"What I'm talking about is don't ask me to play lacrosse in the middle of lunch just to show off. The girls here don't want you and that wacky hair, bro." Jim gave me a hateful grin.

Andy and his friends howled, clutching their sides as they convulsed in fits of laughter. The girls at my table looked at me in confusion and horror.

I was irate. "Are you kidding me? Are you really doing this to me?" I asked Jim. "How can you switch up like that?"

"Relax, bro. Just because we're on the same lacrosse team doesn't make us friends," Jim scoffed.

And just like that, our friendship was over. Jim joined the popular crowd with Andy. Soon enough, the rest of the new kids picked up on the social cues and joined the bandwagon. They refused to hang out with me. My efforts to keep my unpopular past under cover were all in vain. I found myself sitting alone at lunch once again. There were times when I didn't understand the point of living. Why continue existing if every waking moment was hell?

That school year was the most painful year of my life, maybe because I felt like the Fates had cruelly teased me by showing me how fun life could be with friends. But that was never meant to be. Before we were even halfway through the school year, Jim, Andy, and their slew of friends started humiliating me every day in the cafeteria in front of the girls, and it got so bad that I was no longer able to eat there. I started eating in the library.

The contagion spread to the rest of the school. Tenth and eleventh graders I'd never met greeted me in the hallways by saying, "Wassup, Oreo?" Some mocked the way I walked, thrusting their chests out and holding their arms at stiff angles. Many days I walked to the very last shelf in the library, where nobody could see me, and I wept tears of absolute rage. I hated my life, and I was irate that I had to live it. *What did I do to deserve all of this?*

I was so desperate to be liked that I changed my voicemail to create the illusion that I had friends. "Thank you for calling," I said, then I played an audio track of a bunch of guys fooling around and laughing. I pretended that they were the voices of my friends interrupting me, and I said, "Chill," and, "Calm down, bro."

That's when Mommy and Daddy made the executive

decision to send me to live with Uncle Arnold in Nigeria, where I'd finish high school. Switching private schools was no longer an option because the private school community was very small, and I'd probably end up back at square one wherever I went. Most of my wealthy classmates had friends in almost every other private school in Maryland. Some of them had even switched schools, which meant that there was no safe option for me in the area.

Before I knew it, I was getting a cocktail of vaccinations in preparation for my trip—shots for yellow fever, typhoid, and hepatitis A. I also had to take pills to prevent malaria. I'd be lying if I said I wasn't scared. It seemed I was about to move to a place where it would be very easy to die.

Mommy instructed me to keep a journal.

Last lacrosse game before leaving America

6
_____

YOU WHITE RAT

Stepping off the plane in Lagos International Airport with my father and my brother, I slammed face-first into a wall of hot air and body odor. *What kind of a nasty place is this?* This was my introduction to Lagos, a place where none of the public toilet stalls had toilet paper and the same Elvis record played on infinite repeat all year round. I was worlds away from skate parks and lacrosse fields.

One of Uncle Arnold's warnings about the airport was that several people would pose as the driver he'd sent to pick us up. He told us to ignore them and to look for the man named Mr. Wisdom. We were the only people there with white skin, and foreigners in Nigeria were a natural target for scams, burglary, and, on occasion, kidnapping.

As my father, brother, and I walked outside to wait for Mr. Wisdom, a dark man with tribal marks scarred into his face approached us and told us that he would convert our money for us free of charge. He held up a 100-naira note and asked us for a 100 dollar bill. Unfortunately for him, we were smart enough to know that one US dollar was the equivalent of 150 naira. This blatant attempt of theft was rather eye-opening considering that we'd only stepped a few feet from the sliding doors of the airport lobby.

While I searched up and down the circular drive of the airport entrance, my eyes met with unfamiliar faces, who either beckoned me to come to them or shouted, "*Oyinbo pepe!*" My father later informed me that the words translated into "extra-white man." Great. The racist slurs had begun already.

After about fifteen minutes, our driver arrived and greeted us with vice-grip handshakes. He put our luggage into the trunk, opened the rear passenger doors, and invited us to climb in.

On the way to Uncle's house, I took note of several startling realities: it was legal to burn large piles of trash roadside, people gave us the "*wakka*" (a five-fingered equivalent of the middle finger) for taking pictures of them from the car, and there were no traffic lights.

"Wakka" *insult*

Trash about to be burned along the road

Haze over the town from burning trash

Motorbikes called *"okada"* zipped between cars in traffic, carrying three or four people at a time, the rear passenger dangling precariously close to the edge of the seat. I hadn't thought it physically possible to fit that many people on a two-wheeled vehicle. Most of the passengers either carried baskets or bulging plastic bags on their heads.

Four people scrambling to board an okada *taxi*

One of countless okada *accidents*

Some items people carried on an okada

An okada *speeding between vehicles while carrying passengers*

As our car approached one of the larger intersections, the flow of traffic slowed to a halt. Out of nowhere, a machine-gun wielding man in an official uniform and a beret stepped in front of our car and signaled for us to stop. Frightened, I asked Mr. Wisdom if we were in trouble.

"No, they just want their bribe," he said.

My father instructed me to keep my mouth quiet as the crooked police officer climbed into our car and pointed out a dirt path off the side of the road, which he wanted us to drive down. The vehicle instantly filled with an unbearable stench of sun-baked armpit and moldy sweat. Mr. Wisdom methodically pulled out a stack of naira notes and handed it to the smelly man. And just like that, he got out of our car and motioned for us to continue our journey.

Mr. Wisdom said, "It is because he sees *oyinbo* man. This is the reason it is important for you to stay in the backseat, where the police are less likely to see you. In this country, white skin means money, and they will throw you in jail if you do not comply."

I was partly horrified and partly impressed with Mr. Wisdom's expertise.

Corrupt police blocking traffic and demanding bribes

Officer approaching our car

The abysmal traffic and road conditions turned the fifteen-mile trip from the airport to Uncle's house into a two-and-a-half-hour trek. During our overland expedition, I saw people hitching rides on anything with an engine. I also discovered ghastly potholes large enough to total a speeding van. Mr. Wisdom explained just how dangerous the potholes were in ways we couldn't have imagined. When it rained, he told us, the water made holes that were more than two feet deep appear level with the surface of the road.

Trash truck taxi

Taxi van with passenger standing in the door. The car in the distance is reversing into oncoming traffic.

People carried just about anything on their heads

Marketplace stalls and vendors bore no resemblance to those in America

Food sold directly above sewage-filled gutters

Marketplace with a chicken running across the road in the distance

When we were finally in Uncle's neighborhood, we slowly snaked our way down various dirt roads before hitting a long cement strip. Following the cement road, I looked to the left and to the right of our path and saw nine-foot concrete walls with barbed wire, topped with broken bottles that were cemented in place, sharp edges upward. These broken bottles made up what they called the "anti-burglar." When we were in front of the house, a twenty-foot black iron gate slid open. It was powered by a gateman, who welcomed us. This was Uncle Arnold's compound, a 6,000-square-foot concrete fortress in the middle of a two-acre plot of land. The house was beautifully designed and visibly reinforced. Steel bars ran across all doors and windows. I carefully inspected the sand-covered landscape. Anchored into the ground a few feet from the front gate sat a massive, diesel-powered generator the size of a small dump-truck. Energy for weeks.

We hadn't driven more than ten feet down the driveway when, out of nowhere, a humongous, 170-pound German Shepard flew around the corner of the house, barking ferociously.

"That is Barkley," Mr. Wisdom informed us. "He is extremely vicious, and you mustn't get out of the car until he is on his leash."

The gateman scrambled to chain Barkley to one of the concrete pillars on the front porch as Mr. Wisdom parked the car.

Uncle's house. White generator on the far right.

Lizard crawling through "anti-burglar" atop a concrete wall

Aunt Adamma, Uncle Arnold's wife, came outside to greet us. She planted a big kiss on my cheek. We followed her into my new home. The sweet aroma of fried plantains and *jollof* rice filled my nostrils.

When we walked into the kitchen, Aunt Adamma said, "This is your Aunt Flora."

Standing before me was Adamma's sister, a short woman in her forties. She wore gold-rimmed glasses.

"Pleased to meet you, Auntie," I said in greeting.

"You too. Welcome to the home," she responded.

Flora was from Port Harcourt, a state approximately two hours from Victoria Island by plane. She was living with Aunt Adamma and Uncle Arnold because she didn't have a job or a husband to support her. She didn't have any children either.

"Ogadi! Come, my dear," Aunt Adamma called to the house girl, who was apparently sweeping the downstairs living room. Within a few seconds, I saw the gentle-faced, twenty-four-year-old house girl, who curtsied as I stretched out my hand to shake hers.

"Drew, Ogadi will cook for you, and so will your Auntie Flora," Aunt Adamma informed me.

"That's very gracious of you. Thank you in advance," I replied.

Ogadi had recently replaced a house girl whom the guard dog, Barkley, had nearly killed. In the coming days, I would hear several stories that involved Barkley attacking visitors to the compound. What set the attack against the house girl apart from the others was that Barkley had clamped down on her neck, refusing to let go.

From the kitchen, Aunt Adamma led my father and me up the marble staircase and through a large, bulletproof door that separated the upstairs bedrooms from the rest of the house. She walked through a second living room, then opened one of the six bedrooms, each of which had its own full bathroom. This house was much larger than our suburban home back in the States. There really was no comparison.

I realized that it would be impossible for anybody to get in or out of the house if it were on lockdown. I would come to learn that these were the security standards implemented in all Nigerian homes.

I walked over to the air conditioning unit mounted in the wall and brought my face close to it, cherishing its relieving breeze. It was just as satisfying as a cold drink of water after trudging through the desert all day.

Aunt Adamma began to go down the list of things to keep in mind: "First off, *never* drink the tap water," she said firmly. Although the compound had its own distillation system and a 2,000-gallon water tank behind the house, we still had to take the necessary precaution of boiling all water before ingesting it. The only exceptions were showering and brushing teeth. Violating that rule would likely yield a case of typhoid fever. "Last month, twenty-five innocent young children died in our town after drinking stream water heavily contaminated with lead," she added.

Wow.

"Secondly, keep all screens closed, especially at night," she continued. "The mosquitos here carry malaria, as you already know."

To the locals, malaria was common and roughly the equivalent of the flu. To foreigners, however, it was an existential threat. I thought I was safe because I'd started taking anti-malarial medication prior to coming to Nigeria, but I would come to find out that the drugs would only be effective for a few weeks. After that, an incident would be almost inevitable.

"Thirdly, never plug in your electronic devices unless the generator is running. Nigeria's power-holding companies are extremely corrupt, and if there is any electricity, it will likely only be at half current. This will undoubtedly ruin anything that is not connected to a surge protector," Aunt Adamma explained.

The list of rules left my stomach in knots. It seemed that nearly every aspect of everyday living was full of peril. There were so many ways to die here. The dog. Drinking water. Insects. It all made my head spin.

Water tank for the compound

It was now close to 7 pm when she finished reviewing the rules. Night had begun to fall, and dinner was to be served in just a few minutes. I was in my room, unpacking my clothes when the lights suddenly went out. I stopped dead in my tracks, unsure of what to do. I made my way downstairs to join my father and everyone else talking in the dining room. They were already holding lanterns. Aunt Flora went outside to turn on the generator. A deep stuttering sound preceded the diesel engine's low hum, which came to life within fifteen seconds. Flora yanked its large switch to the "run" position, and we had electricity. This place was unlike anything I'd ever experienced.

The next morning, I woke up and walked downstairs, where the family was already gathered in the kitchen.

"*Oya*, Drew, come and drink your cereal," Aunt Adamma told me as I greeted everyone. ("*Oya*" means roughly "all right now")

She handed me a jar of sugar cubes and a bowl containing powdered milk. Apparently I was supposed to mix this with water before pouring in the corn flakes.

That day I came to a few more shocking realizations: clothes and dishes were washed by hand here, we weren't permitted to leave the compound, and the neighbors (some of whom lived in small huts) disposed of all their garbage by burning it in their yards. Those fire sent ash and little bits of plastic raining down from the sky, and they clung to the screens over our windows.

My brother and father stayed with me for two more weeks before departing back to America. For the remainder of their stay, we always either had the generator running, or there was just enough electricity to allow us to use the air conditioners. That all changed as soon as they left.

Once my father and Micah weren't around, Aunt Flora revealed that she didn't like me in the least. I woke up around 9 am, drenched with sweat in the stale, eighty-five-degree air. The generator had been switched off as soon as Aunt Adamma and Uncle Arnold left for work a few hours earlier.

I walked downstairs to the living room and greeted Flora, "Good morning, Auntie."

Without turning to acknowledge me, she mumbled a barely audible response.

"It's quite hot. Can we turn on the generator so we may use the A/C?" I asked her.

As if dodging a wasp, Flora spun around spastically and squinted her eyes, snapping "No way, boy! You go get used to Naija by force, don't worry! I don't know where you think you are."

Confused and slightly annoyed, I silently walked out of the room. I figured I might make mention of Flora's outburst later that evening to Uncle Arnold, but for now I needed to escape the heat of the house by going outside, where at least there was a breeze. At that point, Barkley was accustomed to my presence, so wandering outside wasn't quite as fraught with danger as it had been when I first arrived.

I realized that it might be a challenge being stuck at home with Flora by myself every day because Auntie Adamma and Uncle Arnold left early in the morning for work, and they didn't return until evening. Flora instructed the house girl to wash only Aunt Adamma's, Uncle Arnold's, and her clothes. I had to wash mine by myself. She also told the girl not to listen to anything I asked her do to, which was very little in any case.

By around 10:30 that morning, I was ready to take my morning shower, but I discovered I was out of toiletries. I asked Flora where I could find soap, but she ignored me. I stood quietly for a moment, hoping that perhaps she hadn't heard me, but I suspected that she was ignoring me. I waited for an uncomfortable twenty seconds, standing awkwardly in the living room. Then I dared to ask again.

"Please, Aunt Flora, where may I find soap?"

"*Oyinbo* man, what is wrong with you?!" she screamed. "Didn't Uncle give you what you needed before he left? Why are you bothering me?"

"I'm so sorry," I said as respectfully as possible. "I didn't mean to annoy you, but Uncle instructed me to ask you for anything I need in the house."

Flora stormed up the stairs, returning a minute later with the same bar soap the house girl used for washing clothes. She threw it at my feet. "Here is B-28 multipurpose soap. I don't want to hear another word from your white head," she barked.

I reluctantly picked up the multipurpose bar, wondering why she was treating me so cruelly. I also needed shampoo and a towel, but I knew better than to ask. I suddenly remembered the storage room on the upper level. Deciding to be self-sufficient, I walked upstairs to the closed door of the storage room. Cautiously, I opened it and began searching for toiletries. Within minutes, I heard a rustling behind me.

"What the hell are you doing in here?!" Flora screeched. "So, we have a proper thief in the house! *Ole*, you wicked fool," ("*Ole*" translates to "thief").

I looked at her in disbelief. This was my uncle's house, not a prison. Surely I was allowed to use items from storage just like everybody else. "Please, Auntie," I started, "I'm just looking for shampoo."

"Shampoo for where? Shampoo for why? This is not what you think it is, you spoiled buffoon! Just let me catch you in here again, and you will see what happens to you, you white rat." She jabbed a finger at me. "I will call my brothers to come over here and beat you severely."

Flora shoved me out of the storage and slammed the door viciously. I retreated to my bathroom, climbed into the shower, and angrily lathered myself with the odd smelling B-28 multipurpose laundry soap. I dried off with one of my undershirts.

I spent the rest of the day avoiding Flora, which meant that I had no meals until Uncle came home at 7 that evening. I had dinner with him.

When the generator was shut off at 10 that night, I got ready for bed using light from the candles I had stuck to the floor. Then I dropped to my knees. I prayed that the Lord would deliver me from Flora, the satanic woman I'd have to spend the next weeks with, alone. I couldn't for the life of me understand why she hated me, but I figured that it might have something to do with my skin tone. She continually referred to me as a "white man" and a "white rat."

I struggled to fall sleep in the humid eighty-five-degree room. I was tempted to open the windows, but I feared that the deadly mosquitoes would somehow wiggle their way in through the screens. Tons of them accumulated on the screens just minutes after I opened the window. It was something straight out of a nightmare.

7

BARKLEY THE KILLER

Barkley reigned supreme within the fortified walls of my uncle's two-acre compound. That mutt loved to kill— snakes, lizards, other dogs, and pretty much anything unfortunate enough to drop over the nine-foot-high concrete walls surrounding the compound. Human beings weren't exempt. Luckily, the people who had faced Barkley's wrath had been saved from the jaws of death. That included one of my uncle's former maids, who had apparently been stealing from the kitchen. One day as she was leaving with food clutched firmly to her bosom, and Barkley somehow sensed that she was a thief. He dragged her across the yard by her shoulder. Needless to say, she never returned to work at the compound.

The stifling tropical heat of Victoria Island made life without electricity absolutely unbearable. I grew to deeply resent the fact that we could only turn on the power once my aunt and uncle had returned from work, around 6 in the evening. That meant that I spent the entire day outside in eighty- or ninety-degree weather because that was marginally more comfortable than the stifling air in the sun-baked house.

Barkley liked to play fetch with stones. If you launched a pebble 250 feet across the front yard, he would find that very stone, regardless of where it landed in the sand, and bring it back to you. I enjoyed playing with him, except that he seemed to suffer from some sort of multiple-personality disorder. Exactly thirty minutes after I started playing with him, he would stop dead in his tracks, and the fur on his back would stand straight up as he began to growl. It was the eeriest thing.

One Saturday morning, I was hand washing all of my clothing in the basins outside with a bar of B-28, just as I did every weekend. For some reason, Barkley kept putting his nose into the basin full of soap bubbles and clean clothes. I shooed him away several times, but he continued to circle back around and dip his nose into the bubble. The final time I shooed him, he began growling viciously. He stood motionless, staring at me, baring his teeth. Then he turned and walked about forty feet to the water tower.

Hoping to cheer him up, I picked up a few of his favorite pebbles lying on the ground. "Here, boy! Let's play catch," I called to him. I walked over to where he was lying down. When I was about ten feet from him, Barkley sprang up and charged me in a savage rage. Terrified, I stumbled backward and tripped over the concrete slab covering the septic tank in the middle of the yard, falling flat on my back. Barkley immediately went for my neck. I instinctually raised my left arm to shield myself. His teeth sank deep into the flesh of my forearm, which was right over my neck. I realized that he was trying to kill me.

Frantic, I jammed my right middle finger into his eye socket, but that didn't faze him. I dug my finger in, hoping I could scoop out one of the demon's eyeballs. He whipped his head back and forth, tearing deeper into my arm with each bite. After what seemed like an eternity, Mr. Wisdom came flying out of the house. He grabbed the dog, but Barkley wouldn't let go. Mr. Wisdom beat the dog over the head with a broomstick until it broke. It took a superhuman effort for the driver to finally pry the possessed creature from my arm. When I was finally free, I stumbled to my feet and ran into the house.

Looking down at my mangled limb, I saw yellow fatty tissue hanging from several gaping wounds in my left arm, and my right wrist was slashed severely. I hadn't even realized that he'd bitten my right hand. I began to cry for my mother. I was distraught and alone in a foreign land of endless perils, and I just wanted my mommy.

Aunt Flora came downstairs to see what all the commotion was about. She took one look at me, and she had to stifle a laugh. "So, the dog has dealt with you, eh," she muttered, half grinning.

Minutes later, Mr. Wisdom rushed me to the local Chevron hospital, where it became painfully obvious how poor healthcare was in Nigeria. Rather than sewing the gashes in my arm and wrist, they stuffed the wounds with ointment and gauze. The horrid scars that I carry with me to this day are proof of the incompetence of the nurses and "doctors" at that hospital. In Nigeria and much of Africa, doctors often pay their way through West African medical schools rather than earning their titles by merit. I paid the price for that corrupt system.

Arm and hand mangled from bites

Suffering in my humid, ninety-degree bedroom

8

FLORA

I wrote this letter to my parents under extreme duress:

Dear Mommy and Daddy,

You have known me all my life. You know that I'm not perfect but still a good child. You are also aware that the bond of trust between us is very strong; I never lie to you nor withhold information from you.

Throughout my stay in Nigeria, I've been under intense pressure. In the very beginning, I was worried about what I might encounter in school; however, I've been faced with a different battle.

I should be at ease in my own uncle's house, but being constantly scolded by Aunt Adamma's miserable sister, Flora, keeps me constantly on edge.

"It's either Flora is insane or you're lying," Uncle Arnold tells me when discussing the relationship between Flora and me. She has him convinced that I am trying to make him give up on me and send me back to the States. I don't know how she convinced him to see me in such an evil light, but I haven't been able to shake this image, and it's dragging me down a path that I don't deserve. I don't know how to keep this woman happy. I obey every single command barked at me in hopes of being granted the benefit of the doubt that I am not a "spoiled American." Though I am careful not to show resentment toward her, Flora labels me "ungrateful, selfish, gluttonous, lazy, sneaky, and wicked" when she complains to Uncle Arnold.

Flora looks for the slightest mistake to justify hatred toward others (e.g., if I forget to hand-wash my plate in the sink immediately following dinner, she calls me "lazy prick" and refuses to talk to me for the next 24 hours). While angry at me, she locks the pantry and supply rooms throughout the house so that I may not obtain snacks while Auntie and Uncle are at work.

I know certain habits of mine may generate frustration in her, and these are the things that I have been desperately trying to change for the sake of peace. Some of these behaviors include getting up after 10 am and forgetting to remove my cup from the dining room table.

Flora derives joy in taking everything as an insult and arbitrarily forcing you to apologize for angering her. There is nothing that this woman doesn't yell about, and the tone in which she addresses whomever she *censures* is very harsh. If you aren't doing exactly what she wants you to do, all hell breaks loose. Flora used to wake up around 4:30 every day to make breakfast for Uncle and assist him in getting ready for work. She would also sweep the house regularly and maintain the kitchen. These are examples of why Uncle sees her as such a hard-working saint. The last two house girls have left because of this hideous lady: one of them was sacked (fired) because Flora falsely accused her of being too lazy despite the fact that she toiled 9 hours each day without rest. The second house girl fled our compound one morning without informing anybody, forcing Uncle to file a "Missing Individual Report" because he cared for her like his own daughter. It turned out that Flora had been beating her when nobody was looking.

Whenever I desire breakfast in the morning, Flora gives me grief when I ask her for the key to the locked pantry that she has hidden under her mattress. Before the house girl left, Flora yelled at me anytime I asked for food that was locked away, referring me to the house girl. She would always ask me if I thought she looked like a house girl, yet somehow forgot the fact that Uncle had instructed her to provide me food from the very beginning.

I remember a time when my rice didn't have enough stew and I asked Flora for more. She said there was none, but since she had lied to me in the past on multiple occasions, I was highly skeptical. When I checked for myself, I found several gallon buckets of stew that Uncle had purchased. Flora is just a squatter with zero income, so I never understood why she randomly restricted me from my uncle's resources. The whole thing is a power trip. I removed the stew from the fridge and served myself. Upon discovering that I had uncovered her lie, she went into an animalistic rage, similar to that of a rabid hyena. She called me a stupid white thief. She told me that my parents had abandoned me and that nobody in the world liked an ugly white man who had a black man's hair.

There was a time when Flora refused to speak to me for 3 weeks straight. The cause: I didn't like how she always barged into my room. One day when she stormed in as I was putting on my pants, I asked her, "Please,

99

Auntie, would you mind knocking before entering?" That was all it took. She went ballistic.

"So you are instructing a grown adult not to enter the room of an immature child in her own house!" she roared.

I stood there thinking to myself, *This is not your house, woman.* "But Auntie Flora, even Uncle Arnold knocks before entering my room...he's a grown man, and yet he still has the common courtesy to knock before entering a bedroom," I responded.

The words Flora started hurling at me are too explicit to write to you. Since that day, Flora has intentionally made a point not to knock before entering my room. She began doing so as frequently as possible, even if it was as pointless as walking in and walking right back out. Many times when she enters my room, she doesn't even say a word to me.

I remember the week when Aunt Adamma and Uncle Arnold left for a vacation in Hawaii. I overheard Flora saying that finally she'd be free of cooking and she would be able to rest. About to be the only other person besides her in the house, it wasn't hard to translate the meaning of this comment. Sure enough, that day I had to find myself dinner. There was no light and all food was locked away, so I came to the realization that the situation had reached yet another critical point; if I didn't kiss her butt, I would starve. You see, as soon as my brother and father left Nigeria, Flora arbitrarily decided to permanently lock away all the food in the storage and freezer. This effectively forced me to *consult* her whenever hungry. She knew that it was checkmate for her. After I had finished kissing up to her, she threw a single pack of microwaveable noodles at the floor in front of me.

I had to continually lick Flora's feet (e.g., sweep the

house or clean the table and counters without her asking) in order to get the pantry unlocked for breakfast. Every morning since Uncle and Auntie left has been a struggle and has required a plan of action in order to be able to get breakfast. I remember when she began keeping all the bread inside the locked freezer and taking the milk away from the kitchen so that I wouldn't be able to take cereal at my own will. She also filled the milk container with baking soda one day and didn't tell me, so when I went to go and get milk for my hot chocolate, I got a nasty surprise and had to pour everything away. I also remember when she began hiding the TV remote control from me (and it's not as if I frequently watched TV). Additionally, if I was in the middle of a program, she would *grab* the remote from the couch I was sitting on, go downstairs, and change the channel to whatever she wanted to watch. I would quietly go into my room and continue to study as I was doing before I had settled down for a little break.

The other day this exact thing happened, and I decided to let an hour pass before I did something about it. I eventually walked downstairs and found her on the couch, pretending to sleep. I knew she was only pretending so as to find out whether or not I was going to take the remote. When I picked up the remote, she opened her eyes in an immediate scowl, similar to that of a dangerous troll. Flora began yelling, "You are a very stupid fool." I left her alone with the remote.

For the next couple of days, Flora kept the remote in her room whenever she wasn't watching.

When my 5-year-old niece Isie and 3-year-old nephew Ike (cousin Amadi's children) stayed in the house with us for a couple of weeks, Flora used it as an opportunity to show me what I was missing: she would give them ice cream, apples, chocolate, cupcakes, special cereal, make pancakes and eggs for them every day—then have them eat it in front of me. Whenever I would talk to Isie or Ike or give them a direction and Flora happened to overhear, she would either a) snarl at me ("Who do you think you are?") in front of the children or b) counter what I had said to them, immediately undermining my words. Sometimes I would respond to her in anger, saying, "I'm their biological uncle, thanks for asking." Hopefully that got the point across that she wasn't their real blood, but I doubt it registered. "They are not related to any bright yellow demon, my friend," she would yap at me.

Flora has Uncle Arnold under her spell. He thinks that she is a wonderful woman simply because she treats him with utmost respect for allowing her to squat in his house for years on end. When I complain to Uncle, he responds with statements like, "She cooks for you every day." This is entirely untrue, but I don't think he is aware of the extent of her wickedness. I cannot be mad at him; he took me under his wing and treats me as a son. He works so hard, which also means he is never at the house except Saturdays and Sundays; how would the poor man really understand my strife? Over the last 6 months, the occasions Flora cooked a meal for me could be counted on one hand. She shows me disdain and hatred at every opportunity, but after listening to all her twisted lies about me, Uncle conveys to Daddy over the phone that Flora is a tolerant and loving mother figure. From what Flora tells him, Uncle Arnold thinks I derive joy from making people angry.

Today, on October 27, 2007, I had just entered the kitchen, when she told me I should go and clean the pot with which the house girl had just cooked my spaghetti. Since the kitchen sink was being used by the house girl, I waited upstairs for five minutes, then came back down. I couldn't find the pot, so I asked her, "Auntie, where's the pot you wanted me to clean?" She ignored me, which is her typical response after she's given me a set of instructions and I ask her any question. I felt so angry and embarrassed, as other people were in the kitchen listening to the conversation (or more like monologue) and she was making me look stupid. I asked her again where I could find the pot, but again she didn't respond, so I left the kitchen. On my way out, she began yapping away in Igbo, and I have no idea what she said, but it was obviously something extremely derogatory directed toward me.

Many times when we are in the presence of other people from outside the house and I ask Flora a question, she will ignore me and make me look like a house boy of some sort. Similar behavior was exemplified by a time when I was about to start boarding school and Aunt Adamma had Flora escort me to a local shop to buy shampoo and powder. Flora walked into the shop ahead of me before I could even get out of the car. When I entered the shop, she led me to the detergent section and asked me to hurry up and pick something. Recognizing that she was too bush (primitive) to realize that we were in the kitchen section, I informed her we were in the wrong section of the store. She hesitated for a fleeting moment, then insisted in an exasperated manner that I purchase what turned out to be concentrated dishwasher soap. When I refused and walked over to the shampoo section, she began yelling at me to hurry up and not waste her time.

This was confusing to me, bearing in mind the fact that we were there for ME...Once again, she just wanted to appear as though she had something more important to do.

Flora loves to hate people; thus, it is all too easy to get on her bad side. She doesn't have an ounce of forgiveness in her heart. She is an unmarried 40-something-year-old woman with a beard and without kids. She never shaves her face. She hates the American way of raising a family, and from the way she talks, I was able to conclude that she thinks my mom is some sort of white trash who has a dysfunctional family. This alone could make me hate her for life.

Uncle Arnold and Aunt Adamma leave the house in the early hours of the morning (from 4:30 to 5:30). For the remainder of the day, I am home with Flora, and nobody **ever** sees what goes on...Flora is the embodiment of Satan. Being under her rule all day, every day leaves me depressed in my own home. She constantly lies to Uncle Arnold that I am insolent. For example, Flora expects me to sweep the dining room and kitchen every day at 9 am. If I am late by 1 minute, she goes into an uncontrollable rage of screaming and cursing. My apologies to her are rejected, so I have recently started walking away from her while she yells. Flora reports to Uncle, saying that I consistently walk away from her in defiance whenever she gently corrects me.

I am unhappy with my situation in life, miss home, feel depressed because I haven't any friends, and all my skills seem to be slipping away. I really don't know if I can bear this pain any longer.

I long for harmony, but Flora does not believe in burying the hatchet. If I make a mistake on Monday, Flora will display her disdain for me until Wednesday. I find it hard to forgive her for never showing me empathy or compassion. For some reason, Flora thinks that acting like a mindless drill sergeant every day is the best way to run a home. When I go to report to uncle that I am having trouble with Auntie Flora, he begins to lecture me about how my disrespect caused all of it. On a nightly basis, I retreat to my room and pray that the Lord rescues me from this situation, allows the truth to prevail, and helps me tolerate Flora.

Flora accuses me of making calls to my parents and lying in what I say to you guys. On several occasions, Flora mockingly told me to "go and phone your white mother and father if you don't like what I have said." She knows she has pushed Uncle Arnold to a point where he will not believe my word against hers.

The other day, Uncle was speaking over the phone with Dad and conveying to him my issues with Flora. He put the phone on speaker and had myself and Flora stand next to him as my father began ranting about how my life still hasn't changed, and how when I was 7 I had consistent issues at summer camp where somebody wanted to "kill" me. He went on to mention how throughout my schooling, I've had problems with classmates, and then instructed me to immediately go and kneel in front of Flora and beg for forgiveness. Flora stared at me with a defiant smile of triumph that I tried to ignore. As we stood listening to the conversation, I would occasionally meet eyes with her, and Flora would throw a fit, telling uncle that I was insulting her again. This would cause Uncle to reprimand me mid-conversation to my dad's hearing. Encouraged by his scolding, she went on to talk about how she was going to bring boys to the house to "beat me well." I responded to her and told her that she could go ahead and do just that, and we would see what would happen to them. This was not the only time she threatened to bring people to the house to do me in; not too long ago, she said she was going to call her younger brothers to come and brush (severely beat) me in the compound.

This house is a living hell for me. You wouldn't believe that Flora calls herself a deep Christian. She goes for "night vigils" and thinks she's some sort of untouchable mystic, but you should hear the way she speaks to our driver and house help, Mr. Wisdom. He is one of the most humble men I have ever met, yet Flora scolds him like a stray dog and constantly dehumanizes him.

She locks the kitchen at night, keeps all the toilet paper in her room so that I'm forced to ask her before taking some, and locks the extension to Uncle's room during the day as though I'm a thief who steals from his family members.

There are so many more things that I should mention, but they are escaping my memory right now. I am never able to tell you everything I want to when we speak over the phone, and often Flora will stand on the stairs listening to our conversation so that she can use my words against me later on. I'm so sick and tired of writing about this witch, but I'm hoping it will shed some light on who she is so that you are not disappointed in me when Uncle calls you to report. He never gives me a chance to explain to him what she does to me because I am viewed as the child, and the adult is always right. If you were here to see what goes on, you would hate her more than the dog that scarred my arm.

Love,

Drew

9

SNOWBALL

The stagnant months between my arrival in Nigeria and the start of the school year at Whitesands Boarding School left me eager for a new beginning. Life at my uncle's compound felt like prison. Without electricity, the house was sweltering, and it wasn't much cooler outside. And my demonic prison guard yelled at me constantly. It was no place for a child.

On the day of my departure to Whitesands, I'd packed several suitcases full of clothing, toiletries, and books. Mr. Wisdom drove for nearly two hours before we arrived at the hostel, a large, concrete building encircled by a barbed-wire fence. Menacing jail bars were bolted over every door and window. It's hard to imagine a less inviting place.

As I joined a line of boys waiting with their belongings inside the boarding house, a man I would come to know as Mr. Alabi yelled across the room to check us in. The boarding house mother, Ms. Johnson, stood in the middle of the parlor, silently staring at everybody, her arms crossed at her chest, an expression of disdain darkening her face. I quickly came to learn just how strict boarding house life was going to be when Mr. Alabi ripped through the suit-cases of a boy in front of me, searching for "contraband," throwing clothes all over the floor in the process.

When he extracted a hidden bag of candy, he roared, "Stupid booooy! What is the meaning of this?" He wore a scowl and a half smile at the same time.

"Please, sir, that is just my snack," the boy responded.

"You must be very stupid, upon mad, upon stupid again!" barked Mr. Alabi. He marched swiftly across the room to a trashcan, held the candy high over his head, and slammed it into the garbage with all his might. "Your candy is in a better place, my friend!" He laughed maniacally. Returning to the boy's suitcase, Mr. Alabi dumped every-thing out on the ground.

Ms. Johnson, the divorced mother of one of the seniors, was short and fair-skinned. She'd earned a reputation as one of the strictest, most callous members of the faculty at the hostel. She was known to issue severe punishments such as hour-long sessions of kneeling on stones, whippings, and the withholding of food for even the most minute of infrac-tions. It's possible that her hardened persona came from dealing with the criminals who'd been sent to boarding school at Whitesands over the years. Whatever the reason, she was a wretched person to be around. I'd soon find that out personally.

Mr. Alabi didn't give me any trouble that day because there was nothing in my suitcases except books, toiletries, and clothes. Within minutes, I was on my way upstairs to the bedrooms. The upper level was divided into three main rooms with bunks and two shower areas. I walked into the first bedroom and selected a bunk bed, then I began unpacking along with the other boys who had completed check-in. Conversations sprang up all over the room. A few of the boys asked me where I was from. Another asked me how I ended up in Nigeria. I kept my answers short and friendly, fully aware that giving too much information could quickly transform curiosity into hatred.

Once everybody had checked in, we found that there were approximately thirty boys upstairs. I was the only person with white skin in the entire boarding house, but that didn't bother me. Later that evening at dinner, I noticed several people glancing at me, some more than once. I was clearly an unusual sight. After dinner, we all retired upstairs for bed, around 9. I noticed that I was one of only two boys who had showered and brushed his teeth.

When I climbed into bed that night, I was thrilled to hear the generator running because it meant that I'd be able to sleep in a room cooler than eighty degrees. I wondered why my wealthy uncle was so cheap, why he didn't run the generator through the night back at home. But I wasn't mad at him as I drifted off to sleep.

The next morning started at 6, when we were awoken by a large bell being viciously rung in our rooms. People instantly began to que for the showers. There were thirty boys in line for six showers, which meant a long wait for everyone, and I was among the last in line. I learned that morning that I had to have my bed made and my shoes arranged properly underneath it to pass Mr. Alabi's inspection. If we passed, Mr. Alabi handed us a small, carnival-type ticket ("Admit One"), which we had to present to Ms. Johnson downstairs to get breakfast. It was hard to wrap my mind around the meal situation. No matter how hungry you were, you needed permission to eat.

Once I was finally finished getting ready upstairs, I brought my ticket downstairs to the kitchen.

"Good morning, ma'am," I said to an already irritated Ms. Johnson, holding out my meal ticket to her.

"Andrew, what do you think you are doing?" she growled.

I had no idea what she was talking about. "Sorry?"

"You must be very stupid to think that you can eat your breakfast without dressing up properly. Go back upstairs. Tuck in your shirt, do your tie, then come back down," she snapped.

"Ok, no worries," I replied.

"Shut your mouth!" she barked. "There is no need to have the last word in my boarding house."

As I left the kitchen, anger became anxiety and then hopelessness. I really was a prisoner.

That day at school, I encountered even more intrigued stares from other boys. I came to the terrifying realization that I lacked experience in subjects in which my classmates had a two-year head start on me, including physics and chemistry, both of which were advanced and assumed high competency and ample prior knowledge. Equally worrying was the fact that I found it extremely difficult to understand what many of my teachers were saying, so thick were their accents.

The language barrier was imposing, and it made my first day of school extremely stressful. I often needed help, but I couldn't understand what my instructors said when I asked for clarification. I was relieved when school let out and we returned to the boarding house. The rest of the week wasn't much easier.

Meals at boarding house were generally fine, except for Monday and Wednesday evenings, when they served *eba* and *fufu*, a tasteless, doughy food that is meant to be dipped in a slimy soup called *amala*. As native Nigerians, all the other boys in boarding house had grown up eating those foods, but for me they were so disgusting that I had to make a distress call to Uncle Arnold after skipping dinner for the second time. Uncle arranged with Mr. Alabi a meal plan for me that included rice and stew on Monday nights and bread with stew on Wednesday nights.

The following Monday evening marked the start of my new meal plan. That night, as everybody lined up in the dining room, I sat at the long wooden table, waiting for my food. The cook came out of the kitchen with a plate of steaming rice and stew and set it down in front of me. The entire room fell silent.

"Are you serious, this guy?" said a boy named Afam, whose fake grin barely hid his rage.

Afam was a large boy who stood at around 6'4", and he weighed well over 200 pounds.

"Wow, dey just bend for *oyinbo* man," said his friend, Bob.

Looking around the room, I saw that most faces were either shocked or flat out annoyed.

After we retired to our rooms that evening, Afam confronted me. He accused me of thinking I was better than he was.

"Where did you get that from?" I asked.

"Shut up, stupid albino!" He swung an enormous back-hand, hitting me directly in the face.

I stood terrified, my nose bleeding. I'd never been involved in a physical altercation, beyond pushing and shoving on the lacrosse field. Other boys crowded into the room, yelling and cheering.

"What the hell was that for, dude?!" I screamed. I was too afraid to hit Afam back because I was certain I'd lose the ensuing fight. I'd soon learn that this was the biggest mistake of my Nigerian experience so far because several other boys in the room noted that I didn't retaliate when struck.

One of the spectators, a boy named Mofe, yelled, "Ayyy, Andrew! The white man doesn't hit back, *abi*?" ("*abi*?" translates to "right?")

"Whatever you say, dude," I snarled, my head spinning. Choking up, I ran downstairs to report the incident to Mr. Alabi.

"*Yepa!* The guy is casting, oh!" said several boys. (translation: "Wow! The guy is tattling!")

Reporting the fight to Mr. Alabi did far more harm than good. As punishment for his punch, Afam was forced to clean all the dishes in the kitchen that night, but that only made his hatred for me burn hotter.

One of my seniors in the room at the time of the incident, a boy named Bolaji, took offense to me "casting" Afam. Bolaji stood at 6'2" and was well respected in school. The next day after the bus returned to the hostel, he cornered me in the upstairs bathroom.

He said in a menacing tone, "This guy, why are you a casting guy now?" (translation: "So now you're a tattletale, huh?")

"What do you mean?" I replied. "Afam deserved to be casted for putting his hands on me. You don't treat people like that."

"This guy, shut up. You are a rat!" Bolaji roared, stepping toward me.

"Get out of my face. I don't need anymore headaches today, dude," I snapped at him.

Before I knew what was happening, Bolaji landed a powerful headbutt to my nose. I began bleeding profusely. I screamed and cursed at him, but I was far too afraid to hit him back. Once again, a crowd of rowdy boys formed in the bathroom, making it difficult for me to leave.

"Damn, Andrew. They done mess you up again, oh!" yelled one of the boys.

The room erupted into a fit of laughter. Several boys were clearly tickled; others just looked on in amusement. I pushed my way out of the bathroom and hurried downstairs to Mr. Alabi's room once again. The shrieks of laughter that followed me shook the walls.

"Cast! Cast! Cast! Cast!" chanted some of the boys from upstairs.

I told Mr. Alabi what had happened. He kept me away from the other boys until the start of dinner.

That was only a temporary solution, though. I soon had another violent run-in with a classmate named Mofe, a fat boy who had mocked me for not hitting Afam back. Mofe was only 5'11", but he weighed close to 230 pounds. He was also mentally challenged and could only read picture books. He attended special education classes on the southern end of campus. He typically got slapped around by anybody who wanted to prove himself as a fighter, and he refused to retaliate.

Mofe's defense mechanism was to become the servant of the most popular bully in the school. He thought that would offer him protection, but it actually made life even more miserable for him because the bullies routinely humiliated Mofe. A few years earlier, one of the larger boys in boarding house urinated into Mofe's mouth as he lay asleep in his bunk bed. Mofe woke up crying, and he had to take a shower in the dark because the generator had been switched off for the night.

Mofe decided to boost his status in the boarding house by bullying me because he realized that there would be no consequences. So the following Monday evening, Mofe taunted me at the table.

"*Oyinbo!* The white man cannot eat normal food. His skin is whiter than his teeth. Stupid snowball," he hissed.

Several of the other boys snickered at his ridiculous remarks. I peered at Mofe, my eyes narrowed, but I said nothing. He smiled at me like it was just a joke.

Half an hour later, we retired to our rooms upstairs. I was sitting on the edge of my bed when Mofe barged into the room.

"Stupid white boy. Stupid white boy. What do you do with a stupid white boy?" he chanted.

"What's your deal anyway, man?" I snapped. "I've done nothing to you, yet for some reason you have some kind of random beef with me."

Mofe thrust his chest out. "Whatever, fam. Let me tell you something: this is Nigeria, not America. You are not safe here. What kind of Black man sounds so stupidly white anyway? Go back and hang with the chess players."

I ignored his nonsense. I got up from my bed and walked across the room to my locker, turning my back on him. As I fiddled with my belongings, Mofe crept up behind me and put me in a headlock, compressing my windpipe, completely blocking my airway. I struggled to get him off me, but at 5'9" and 140 pounds, I stood no chance against his aggression. The other boys in the room watched silently as I started to go blue in the face.

"Help!" I mouthed to one of one of the boys, who

pretended to not understand me. I couldn't breathe for a good forty-five seconds, and sparkling stars glimmered in my peripheral vision as I struggled for air.

Just then, Mr. Alabi burst into the room, stormed over to Mofe, and kicked him in the ribcage. Mofe released me, and I fell to the ground, gasping for air.

No, I told Mr. Alabi. There was no need to report the incident.

As I lay in bed that night, miserable and homesick, I began to reflect on my past. All my life, I'd wanted to be white to escape the hatred of people who looked down on me for being half Black, but now I was in a place where being white was a disadvantage. No matter where I went, I couldn't blend in. When I was in class, I felt like an outcast because everyone around me spoke fluent pidgin, and I didn't know any of their slang. My accent was also foreign to them. That meant that there was no way I was going to be able to flirt with girls. I'd moved to a different continent, but I was still the ugly boy who couldn't make even a single friend. They pegged me as an antisocial nerd. "It seems that you only care for those books," they taunted.

I was angry at everyone, including God. I didn't understand why human beings showered me in hatred just because I looked different. I tried putting myself in their shoes, but I couldn't wrap my head around the idea of disliking somebody for no good reason. None of it made any sense to me.

The next day in school, boys mocked me relentlessly about my scuffle with Mofe, in front of the girls no less. I didn't fire back at them for fear that somebody else would attack me.

The rest of the week was just as bad. I thought the weekend would offer me some respite, but I was sadly mistaken.

On Sunday afternoon, I began feeling slightly nauseated. It got worse as the day progressed, and by bedtime, I felt miserable. I tossed and turned before eventually blacking out. Three hours later, I was spewing vomit all over the dorm room. Panic set in. I had no idea what was wrong, but I suspected that the drinking water was the culprit.

The generator was off for the night, so I picked up my flashlight and stumbled down the pitch-black hallway, toward the bathroom. I fumbled with the faucet handles on the closest sink. I was just about to take a swig when I realized the danger of gulping down typhoid infested tap water. With shaking hands, I turned the faucet off and shuffled back down the hallway toward the stairs, clutching my stomach, searching for water. On my way, I knocked on Mr. Alabi's bedroom door, opposite the dining room entrance.

"Drew, what is wrong?" he asked.

"I don't know. I feel incredibly sick, and my head is pounding," I whispered in a weak voice.

Mr. Alabi told me that I had contracted malaria. He sat me down on the living room couch, quickly got dressed, and walked across our concrete front yard to the gateman's small hut, where the bus driver slept. Twenty minutes later, the bus driver was rushing Mr. Alabi and me to the nearest hospital.

I spent four days in a hospital whose technology, medical devices, equipment, beds, and showers looked like they were straight out of the '70s. Everything was outdated and in poor condition. The staff were inattentive and didn't respond to basic requests, even for water. On the second day of my stay, Uncle Arnold came to visit me. He brought food and drinks, reassuring me that everything was going to be fine and that malaria was common in West Africa. Uncle kept my spirits high for a good three hours, but when he left, I fell into a deep depression brought on not only by my illness but also by the difficulty of my life outside of America. I had no family around me, and the boarding house was full of hooligans who seemed to want to kill me for my skin complexion. I had no friends or allies, and I never felt more alone.

Sitting in that miserable hospital, I remembered advice Mommy had given me before leaving for Nigeria: "Keep a journal. Write in it daily." I pulled a pen and a sheet of paper from my backpack next to the bed, and I started describing my daily routine:

Routine

I often wake up before the 5:30 am "rise and shine" and get ready as quickly as possible to avoid any physical altercation over bathroom space. Often there are fistfights over stolen buckets of hot water; however, usually by the time my peers are entering the showers, I've already finished showering and eating. I catch the earliest bus (departure time 6:40 am) to school. The buses make the morning trip to school a total of 2 more times, once at 7:10 am and finally at 7:40 am. By 6:59 am, I am typically at school and making my way toward the music room in the elementary building. In the music room I practice piano until 7:55 am, then make a dash to the other side of our small campus, where my classroom is located. Madam Uko, a very kind woman is my "form tutor" (homeroom teacher). She takes registration/roll call and then makes her way around the classroom checking and signing our homework diaries to make sure we have been studying. By the end of the day I catch the first 4 pm bus back to hostel, leaving me with a good 45 minutes before the second bus returns. This time is golden to me, as I use it for exercising, the same way a man would in a jail cell. Since there obviously isn't any hint of free weights or exercise equipment, I fill my backpack with as many textbooks as I can and curl it until no longer possible. Push-ups and sit ups are done in between sets with the aim of building up muscle until nobody poses a physical threat to me anymore.

Siesta (naptime) ends at 6:00 pm, marking the start of first prep (study hall), which I always attend although it is not mandatory. Dinner is the most anticipated event of the day, starting at 8:00 pm. Following dinner, I always go upstairs to wash my clothes in buckets. Everybody usually washes clothes on Saturday; however, with this custom also comes the fighting over wash basins and clothesline space. Me knocking out laundry daily helps to lessen my stress on Saturday mornings and relieves me of buildup. Afterwards, I take a shower and brush my teeth in preparation for bedtime, which is usually around 10:45 pm for me. This leaves me feeling well rested by morning. I have found that I like to have quiet time by myself because it allows me to think of home. I have also been successful in utilizing my time wisely; I am hooked on my textbooks because I cannot stand sleeping the daylight hours away like everyone else does.

Friday, October 20, 2006

Dear Micah, Mom, and Dad,

Today, Friday, is the first day of my midterm break. I

arrived home from boarding house around 9:05 pm to a pitch-black fortress in Victoria Island; Aunt Adamma and Uncle Arnold were in America, so I would not be seeing them...time to find out if Flora will allow me to turn on the generator. I hope she is in a good mood today...

Electricity within 5 minutes of me requesting—not too bad.

Opening the heavy door to my room upstairs, I found a box sitting on my bed. It said it was from Scotland... actually it didn't say that—but who cares?

Anyways, I think this would be a nice way to "talk" to you guys, seeing that I don't own a cell phone, and typically don't have access to a phone in boarding house. I will eventually mail you guys these notes. I love you so much.

Saturday, October 21, 2006

9:20 pm:

Hey. I'm going to try to make writing these entries a habit. It won't be hard to do in the boarding house because right after school everybody crashes (except me), and I'm left with a 2-hour break during which I don't want to be caught out of my bed. I'm always thinking of my family. I've noticed that whenever I'm stressed out, compositions begin to play in my head. I need to begin writing out some of this music because the melodies are quite pleasant. I wish I had a handheld recording device to hum into. I really don't want to forget the notes.

Peace!

Sunday night, October 29, 2006

Today is my first day returning to boarding house after the midterm break. The junior kids (year 9) are now staying in boarding house with us, adding another 25 to our count. It is so depressing being away from home in such a foreign environment. I often find it extremely difficult to grasp new concepts addressed in our science textbooks, and in seeking assistance from teachers I've become painfully aware of how lazy the instructors are in this place. There is an unmistakable lethargy preventing them from willingly tutoring me without a bribe (or in more polite terms, lesson payment).

All I can think of is how much I love you guys. I know that I am on a mission, but sometimes things just make me feel terrible. A jealous senior has been ordering my juniors to disrespect me. He gossips and says false things against me. His name is Bolaji, the same idiot who headbutted me earlier this year. I avoid him at all costs, but if he puts his worthless hands on me again, I will fight full-fledged. I am praying to God, and I am confident that he will deliver me; however, tears begin stinging my eyes every time I think of home. I love you Micah, Mom, and Dad. You're always in my thoughts.

Monday, October 30, 2006

I just came back from school around 1 hour and 10 minutes ago. I went through an exercise routine that I am trying to make an everyday ritual. I brushed my teeth & washed my face afterwards, then spent some time talking with my bunkmate, who does not mind speaking to me when others are not looking. The two of us usually catch the first bus while everyone else in years 10 and 11 are late and take the second bus an hour later.

I am always thinking of God. I am always thinking of my family. I wish I could see you guys. The second bus is now returning to the hostel.

With roommate, removing dried clothes from makeshift clothesline

About 20 minutes pass

The other guys are back. It's siesta time, and for the next 2 hours, I am expected to sleep...dream on (no pun intended). It's 4:30 and I've got work to do. Task #2 complete!

7:52 pm (before dinner)

I am the only year 10 downstairs studying during first prep (prep = study hall). Everyone else who arrived on the second bus is currently sleeping (or actually about to wake up). I cannot escape this looming cloud of sadness. I miss you guys so much, but writing in my journal helps alleviate some of the pain. I love you all. I am going to say some prayers now.

Tuesday, October 31, 2006

6:30 am

I have been awake for 1 and a half hours (30 minutes longer than everyone else). I discovered that the reason the showers and bathrooms are so crammed in the mornings is because most people shower and brush their teeth ONLY in the morning. I don't understand how you can sleep without doing either of these things at night, especially after a long day in the sweltering African sun. A minor detail I've observed is also that they brush before breakfast rather than afterwards...don't worry, I won't change my style. I was the first downstairs to eat breakfast. I run up to brush, get inspected by Mr. Alabi, and then come back downstairs to start writing this. I am sitting right in front of a refreshingly cool A/C that's freezing the small amount of water on my face left from washing. A terrifying discovery I made a few weeks ago was that mosquitos like to hang out in the depths of the air conditioner all night until it is turned on in the morning, at which point they all come streaming out with the air. I just killed 5 of them, and I'm fairly certain there aren't any others. I am now going to pray and start my extra studying before school. It is now 6:41 am.

(PS) Is it Halloween?...People over here don't even know what that is.

6:50 am

I just boarded the earliest bus that takes year 11s to early lessons. I am going to play piano on the elementary school 4th floor for a good 50 minutes. This ride is bumpy. I am seriously concerned about the amount of exercise I am able to get. I am still determined to come back and play professional lacrosse as I study medicine. I am beginning to consider attending Johns Hopkins University. We just pulled in front of the school gates.

Peace.

6:20 pm

Catching first bus home has paid off; Ms. Johnson just punished everyone who came on second bus expecting to sleep and miss first prep, and as a result has given everyone who made first bus double portion in snacks. I just ate 2 meat pies and drank hot chocolate. It's shocking to me how much I now look forward to mealtimes; they are literally the highlights of my day in this lonely, loathsome country.

Wednesday, November 1, 2006

6:51 am

I just missed the earliest bus (this is the bus that transports the SS3 to extra lessons), the one I took yesterday. Unfortunately, this will inevitably cut short my piano playing time. It's a little bit depressing; playing the piano helps me forget about my surroundings in the same way that composing journal entries does.

5:40 pm

I am in my room, and prep will start in a few minutes. Deciding to work out today, I used heavy oak chairs to curl and did several sets of push-ups. The dorm doesn't offer any form of exercise and it is driving me crazy, especially when I think of all the varsity football and lacrosse players across the United States who are mastering their art at this very moment. After washing up, I sat off the side of my bunk bed in deep thought, trying to keep things in perspective. I'm sure the bell will ring any minute—there it is. Today I am on snack duty, meaning one of my classmates and I must serve everybody.

Thursday, November 2, 2006

11:45 am

I am in English class right now, and everybody is yelling and running around. Misbehaving would be an understatement, as the teacher has completely given up and is playing solitaire on her computer. Wait a minute... she was playing solitaire before we entered the classroom. This class presents an extremely easy syllabus that is a clear waste of time for me; learning ESOL (English as a second language) in my second-to-last year of high school scares me. All my classmates from St. Mathicus have advanced SAT vocabulary exercises integrated into their

English classes, so I am at a severe disadvantage in comparison. The British IGCSE exams that we are studying for in Nigeria are a completely different testing system, intense in the fields of biology, chemistry, and physics. I feel like I am being forced to dumb-down my speaking in this country, and I fight not to worry that it may be adversely affecting my grammar. I don't use a third of the vocabulary that I had in the advanced English classes I took in America.

I am incredibly discouraged by how chaotic this classroom is, so I try to make myself feel like a high school student again by doing practice problems and any homework that I can find from my challenging science courses. The teacher obviously sees it as more than difficult to conduct any type of lesson while competing with the noise level in here. This is the same situation in my Business Studies class.

Friday, November 3, 2006

7:23 pm

Right now I am in boarding house, upstairs with all the other SS2, SS3, and A-level students. The SS3 and A-level guys get to stay in the annex, where there are twice as many A/C units; basically a paradise in the jungle. They are currently playing soccer with a tape-bound roll of toilet paper, and you can tell that everyone is REALLY into it. All other students are sleeping in the outer and inner rooms of the senior wing. My bed is located under an A/C that used to saturate the foot of my mattress until just recently...as I am writing, I'm remembering all the summers of fun Micah and I had together. I love that kid. I remember when our soccer practicing would send the ball crashing through Ms. Jeannie's front garden at least twice a week. Poor lady.

Right now I feel like I am experiencing a long stretch of challenges in life, and although they are going to make me mightier, it is still considerably difficult thinking of life in the US not but a few months ago. I remember so much that I miss, but I'm gradually forming an everyday routine that is helping to comfort me and keep me focused on my end goal.

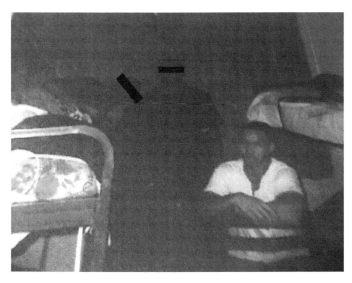

Sitting on heavy oak chair used for curling

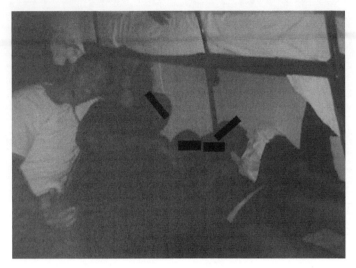

Trying to fraternize

Sunday, November 5, 2006

8:30 pm

Today was...I don't know exactly how to describe it...*horrendous*...One of my juniors lied to the housemaster and got me into trouble, so I had to clear all 50-something plates off the stinking (literally) table. This is the same animal that got me into trouble last week with another disgusting lie that led to me missing socials (free period on Saturdays and Sundays in boarding house, where you can watch TV or make phone calls) and having to weed all this nonsense out of the grass—if you could even call it that. But honestly the start of my day was much worse than anything else. It began at 5:15 am with a vicious splash in the face from Mr. Alabi. See, the problem is that the kids in my room had been talking loudly until 12:45 am, keeping me awake all night. Despite the rude wake-up, I drifted back to sleep. 5 minutes later I received a dirty slap in the middle of my chest from Mr. Alabi, who was just waiting for me to close my eyes.

He then proceeded to slap 4 others awake and shouted for us to follow him downstairs. I was furious—the situation was completely unfair, and now I was running the risk of getting malaria *again*. I threw a fit, and one way or another was allowed to go back to the bunks to get my bug spray. I returned to the group waiting outside, only to be assigned an idiotic task: I was to use a bundled pack of straw to sweep a puddle of water 4 feet in one direction... and then 4 feet back to where it originally formed. I thought to myself, *Is this man intoxicated, or is he really just that bush?* The end result of this assignment left me upstairs, scurrying to get ready for church. I was extremely late, and by the time I was finished with my morning routine, the bus had already left. I was forced to go to "children's church" with my juniors, who jeered at me, saying, "White man is coming with us, oh."

I arrived at church and picked a seat in the back of the room, close to a crumbling cinder block wall. I honestly wanted to sleep, but when push came to shove, I ended up staying awake and alert. The service was painfully slow, as I struggled to appreciate the speaker through his dense village-like accent. As he continued to lecture, I became increasingly aggravated by his shelling (grammatical blunders). For example, rather than saying ,"The other day when we were coming home," the man instead said, "The other day when we were caming home." *CAME-ING IS NOT A WORD!*, I felt like screaming at him. To say that I wasn't downright resentful of the entire situation would be lying; however, I managed to remind myself to focus on the positive. I was starving and could not take my mind off the breakfast that awaited us upon return to the boarding house. Following children's service, I was reunited with my classmates who were on the opposite side of the compound at the adults' worship service. All they could do was laugh at me, and honestly their hysteria made me crack a smile. "Andeyyroo! A.k.a. children's church boy!KAKAKAKA!" they ranted...I began to chuckle. Whatever they said didn't matter: all I wanted was food!

When we returned to hostel, we ended up waiting *2 hours* before having breakfast. I was in agony, and since Mr. Alabi insisted on inspecting our rooms before letting us eat, his lack of urgency was nothing less than a direct attack. We ended up being the last room let downstairs for food, so by the time we got to the table, *the blessed tea was finished*. Following breakfast, we were all assigned our weekly duties. I was on table duty and promptly carried out the task of clearing and washing all the tables. By the time I was done, it was siesta, and I jammed on my chemistry, studying. 2 hours. Later we began preparing for the parents who visit their children in hostel every first Sunday of the month...Since Uncle and Auntie had left Nigeria, I had no visitors.

(PS) Melodies are playing in my head as I write this. These compositions of mine are very catchy.

Waiting for Mr. Alabi to inspect our room

Monday, November 6, 2006

6:05 pm

Tuesday, November 7, 2006

Around 24 hours ago, I started an entry but was unable to finish it because the boarding house master called me away for something...I forget what it was. Anyways, it is now around 6 pm (I am not sure of the actual time because I am not near a clock, and we are forbidden to get up during prep). Surprisingly, today was a good day; a lot of things happened, and my stress level was not high at all. To top it all off, I got to talk to Dad about 45 minutes ago, and we spent 17 minutes on the line. Mr. Alabi got annoyed because I went over the 15-minute mark that he arbitrarily set, but nobody was waiting in line behind me for the phone, and you guys were paying for the call, so I just ignored the idiot's attempts to make me feel guilty (he is the type of power-tripping Nigerian who loves to play stupid games). I really, really want to come home for Christmas. I need to see you guys...I'm so sick and tired of all the wickedness and jealousy shown toward me by so many individuals I have met in this country. Many people in the boarding house categorize me as a rich white kid. They treat me as if I'm trying to push it in their faces that I come from America, but these fools know that I'm not doing anything to them at all—they just like to play games at the expense of others' feelings. One kid named Nnamdi just yapped (insulted) me for a stretch of 5 minutes after butting into a conversation I was having with another American boy, saying that I think I'm the only person who's been to America. He was clearly venting some built-up anger on me, but I simply laughed at him instead of responding negatively. I didn't want a physical altercation, which he would be more than happy to engage me in. I could see the glimmer of hatred in his face as he squinted his eyes to emphasize certain words. What a shame. I am not going to write about that Ms. Johnson wretch. I'll simply talk to you guys over the phone. You will get the letters later.

Thursday, November 9, 2006

3:02 pm (Business Studies class)
    I am very good with my mathematics class and my

Additional Mathematics class...On second thought, I am not going to write right now.

I recently discovered that I am able to draw caricatures quite well. Here are some of my teachers:

5:40 pm

Earlier on I was writing with two people sitting beside me, screaming their heads off, so I decided to just draw instead. The business class is so useless.

7:30 pm

In business class, it is typically so loud that the teacher's voice is drowned out by the never-ending chit-chat. My teacher must just be learning the subject because for the entirety of the "class," he dictates directly from the book, and whenever he tries to branch out and use his own words, it sounds embarrassingly elementary. We honestly aren't even going into any topics relating to business or any of its aspects, as the book seems to have been written for 6th graders; all we do is define terms. Today was stressful from the moment physics class ended. I was not grasping any of the topics being presented, but the other kids in class had already learned parts of it in middle school, so the teacher just breezed through the lesson, assuming that we were all on the same page. After hours of independent study however, I am now beginning to understand things but still must dedicate time for review.

In my chemistry and mathematics classes, the tides have turned for me. Thanks to incredible perseverance, I am now on top of all the material in these courses and able to grasp new concepts very quickly. I feel a lot better than I did 3 weeks ago. I feel an indescribable presence guiding me and keeping my spirits above ground. I miss you guys so much. All I can think of is the prospect of me coming home for Christmas—it would be such a heavenly relief.

There is one thing I am looking forward to: tonight we are eating hamburgers and chips (the British term for slices of fried potato). There isn't any cheese on the burgers though...I can't wait to talk to you guys again.

Friday, November 10, 2006

5:30 pm

This morning the generator malfunctioned and we were left without water or electricity, so as a result, I had to run outside and fetch water from the typhoid-infested tap (reserved exclusively for washing clothes) and use it to brush my teeth. I got to school by means of the first bus, which I narrowly made, and went to practice my piano. I am excited to say that I can now play the first 4 pages of *Rachmaninoff Concerto No.2 in C minor* flawlessly, full speed with both hands, and read my way through the 5th and 6th pages. I am quickly learning the unabridged version of "*How Great Thou Art*" and am beginning to play the full version of *Rachmaninoff Prelude No 4*. Keeping up with my piano skills has been crucial to my maintaining some sense of what life back home feels like.

As I am writing, the bully named Nnamdi just walked into the room. Apparently he had to catch the late bus back to hostel. He is 16 like me, and is just as muscular as I am, but stands about 2 inches taller and couples it with a very aggressive, angry attitude. He constantly challenges me to fights. Upon the several times that we have arm wrestled, he has only won once, and I am pretty sure that this has caused him to permanently hate me. He simply won't leave me alone. I would be lying if I said that his presence didn't make me uneasy. I honestly think the only way I will have peace of mind here is if I somehow regain my karate skills...it is more than necessary in this boarding house. At the forefront of my mind, however, is the fact that I am no longer struggling the same way in my math and chemistry classes. What a relief.

It is now 5:45 pm, and I think I will go meditate before I study.

(PS) Siesta ends at 7:00 pm today, so I have got a lot of time to focus.

Love you guys

Saturday, November 11, 2006

(Prayer/God)

Around 11:00 pm

I'm going to try something different tonight; I will write down my prayers at the moment.

Dear Father, please deliver me from this individual who is a constant stress factor for me. Bless me, as my enemies show their jealousy and hatred toward me for absolutely unjust causes. As this boy attacks me with verbal and physical threats, give me the confidence and incredible emotional strength to not allow it to bother me, even though I'm far from home. Decorate me with your HOLY ARMOR. Let me DEFY THE DARKNESS that tries to consume me whenever I am depressed in the wake of stressful situations. I love you, and I need you, Lord. Please be with me. Forgive all of my sins, Father. I am missing my family terribly; please let me see them soon, Father. Let me soar through my subjects in flying colors. Let my tests reflect the desire I have to become a success. Welcome my desire to be close to you with showers of blessings. Give me strength, Father. I really need you. As I sleep tonight, fill my existence with your heavenly presence; I want to feel your presence. Be with my family. Let us all see unending success in all of our endeavors. Let my brother and I become the professional lacrosse players that we are destined to be before we pursue our high-positioned careers. I am in pain...I need you, Father...answer my prayers. I am a warrior for you, Father. Bless my family and me for all we've gone through. In Jesus' name I pray, Amen.

Sunday, November 12, 2006

12:05 am

It's blazing hot in our room. The A/C has been broken for the past 2 weeks, and I've given up on trying to sleep tonight. The maintenance crew or whomever Ms. Johnson calls for fixing appliances has not responded at all, which is terribly infuriating because now it has become overwhelmingly obvious that nobody in this country takes their job seriously. Everyone is lazy. Everyone is always late. Everyone expects a bribe. I'm currently sitting at the end of the laundry table close to the entrance of the bathroom, and this chair is the same uncomfortable flat wooden type that is used in school. If you don't readjust your seating position every 10 minutes, these chairs make you extremely sore and stiff. I cannot believe that I will be expected to wake up in 5.5 hrs. I am going to write another prayer to comfort me. It really does help.

(Prayer)

Dear Lord God Jesus,

Help me. I don't want to feel lost in this world that is lonely away from home. Give me signs (that I can feel) that indicate a bright future for me—a very VERY successful future for me and the rest of my family. Give me the ability to sleep tonight in this constantly oppressive environment, so far away from all that I have ever known. Father, Ms. Johnson is so cruel and inconsiderate; forgive her and bless me. When she vents her personal anger on me, let it pass over me. Remind me that there is nothing wrong with me. Keep me safe from any form of harm; however, it may try and rear its ugly head. Let those who envy me and hate me for being different not affect my well-being. Forgive them and bless me. Allow me to return to the States a stronger man in every way.

I love you, Father. As I just looked up toward the ceiling, you sent rain cascading down outside. I will sleep now father. Protect me. In Jesus' name I pray, Amen.

Wednesday, November 15, 2006

6:09 pm

Around 20 minutes ago I got into a fight with one of the known boarding house bullies who I typically get along with. His name is Omari, and he stands at 6'6" with a muscular Igbo frame and an extremely violent lifestyle. He loves to pick on the juniors, and if you are not one of the "cool" kids or someone who minds their own business 24/7, you are bound to be picked on too. It started today when an ugly British girl with an equally ugly personality began dissing my accent in school. I didn't chew her out, but I made it clear that I didn't appreciate the way she'd been treating me. This nasty Omari boy happens to be one of her close friends, and proceeded to inform me that if I had beef with that girl, I had beef with him too. He decided that roughhousing me in class was the appropriate route. Although many could have seen it as play fighting, it was unwelcome and intrusive. He knew that I didn't want to engage him physically in front of the whole class, but I had no choice but to roughhouse back because if I backed down I would automatically be the

139

target of further bullying in the future. I was hoping that it would end there, but I knew I would have to deal with more nonsense later on.

After school I caught the first bus. I exercised back at hostel by lifting the heavy wooden chairs, doing jumping jacks, and doing push-ups until my arms ached. I then proceeded to wash my underwear in the shower buckets and then take a shower. As I was hanging my clothes up to dry on the side of my bed, my classmates who took the second bus began to pour in. As soon as Omari entered the room, he walked up to me and asked why I'd been dissing the British girl. He moved closer until he was less than an inch away from my face. I pushed him away and told him that I wasn't in the mood for playing, but he got in my face once again. This repeated itself 3 times over, with him grabbing my hands in the process. I escaped and counter attacked him by using his own weight to push him away from me, and then reiterated that I was not interested in play. He then hit me in the throat...*I could not breathe*...a harsh headlock followed, as everybody in the room watched and egged him on. It took me close to 15 seconds to escape, although it seemed much longer. I shoved him away once again, but he bounced right back in my face, and I had no choice but to grab him by the neck. I hoped that this response would be perceived by onlookers as ample retaliation to not categorize me as a "pussy." I released him almost immediately, but at the same instant he grabbed me with extreme force, putting me into a headlock that was far worse than the one before. It took me twice as long to escape his bind, and by the time I did there was a huge crowd encircling us. As soon as I escaped, he bashed my face into the wall, opening the skin above my left eyebrow and upper right cheek.

Days later, injuries still evident above left eyebrow and upper right cheek

Hearing the commotion, Mr. Alabi finally showed up and sent the two of us downstairs to *tell our sides*. Omari lied to Mr. Alabi, saying that it was all play, but then changed his story. I thought to myself, *How is this happening?* When it was my turn to talk, I told it how it was. We were both allowed to go back upstairs, but I got my books and returned back downstairs to try and study. My neck is burning; I really need to learn karate.

The generator is not working right now, so it is getting quite dark inside even though it is only 6:30 pm. It is extremely hot, I am sweating profusely, and all I can think about is the fact that we get to go home tomorrow (Thursday).

I am happy to say that I got your email, Mommy. Hearing about the business trip to Houston is making me feel very happy—it is good to know that things are progressing for our family, and when I'm so far away, it encourages me and refreshes my spirit. I love you all. I hope to hear from you again soon. I can just barely see what I am writing, and I think it's time to get a drink.

The water that I just drank made me want to throw up; it was very warm and had a shockingly tangy taste. Isn't water supposed to be refreshing? I am going to attempt to study for the rest of the 5 minutes of daylight that I have left. Writing this was a priority, however, as it makes me feel better when I have nobody else to talk to.

It is now 7:10 pm, and the generator is finally on. Yesterday, Mrs. Wilson (the vice principal), Mr. Todd (the principal), and the new boarding house "mother" came to hostel to announce that Ms. Johnson would be leaving for good by the end of the week. Believe it or not, there were tears from some people. I honestly didn't feel either way, seeing that she's never been a considerate human being in the first place. I still hugged her and told her that I would miss her, but this was only in hopes that she'd then allow me to use the computer...which to my surprise she did.

My neck is still hurting from that demon's headlock. I really want to leave this hostel, but I am still eager to see how the new boarding house mother is going to treat us. At this time I really wish I could talk to you. The truth is, I feel like weeping, but no tears are coming. I am sitting in an isolated wing of the dining room (where we have prep) with the A/C blowing cold breeze into my face. I keep thinking of the day that I will be able to return home. I'm working so hard for my grades; I'm not going to let this mission end up being a failure. I love you guys...Off to my books, with my future in mind.

By the way...I have been unable to locate my blazer since Monday, and this is very strange because I *never* misplace my items. Could it have been stolen?

Friday, November 17, 2006

The last week in school has been quite miserable for me. As if it isn't stressful enough that I am in a foreign land where the majority of those I encounter on a daily basis treat me like a self-righteous "white man," I am surrounded by criminals at my school. I now know for a fact that my blazer was fapped (stolen) right from under my nose several days ago and is currently being worn by a thieving student who probably smirks as he walks right past me every day. Our names are sewn into the inside of the collar, so there is literally no way to distinguish one blazer from another unless everybody takes theirs off. I don't think anyone in this school understands what it does to a person when you steal something from them; it's one of the worst feelings you can have knowing that somebody out there has something that is rightfully yours, and likely knows that it is tearing you up on the inside. What is worse is when you have to come to terms with the fact that they have gotten away because you do not know who to link the crime to. Not only is it infuriating, but dwelling on it is also exasperating...yet inevitable.

Today brought me unexpected relief from the lingering annoyance of my stolen blazer. I finally went to Mrs. Wilson in sheer distress to inform her of my situation and expressed to her that whoever the thief was had successfully caused me to be depressed. The next actions of this wonderful woman will never be forgotten: Mrs. Wilson called a massive high school assembly. Everybody from SS1 to SS3 (grades 9-11) lined up according to their homeroom in the courtyard and was ordered to remove their blazers for inspection. Their homeroom teachers were then instructed to methodically go down each line and verify the name sewn into the collar of their blazers. 7 minutes into this exercise, my blazer was found on an extremely ugly thief. The teachers humiliated him in front of the entire school, and then called me to the front to come and collect my blazer.

"*Oya*, Mr. Man," one of them prompted me. "Say what you want to this thief!"

I couldn't contain myself, as was evident in my response: "Look at your dirty life! See your extended head, like molded yam. May God forgive your wretched parents for bringing you into this world."

The entire school roared, and many people collapsed onto the cement laughing. My classmates jumped up and down, slapping each other in uncontrollable fits of hysteria. The teachers were among those laughing the loudest; apparently nobody expected me to speak in broken English and use proper Nigerian expressions/terminology, but after all the time I have spent in this country, I can say I've picked up a thing or two. It felt so good having my blazer back in my possession.

Sunday, November 19, 2006

11:00 pm

Right now I'm on my bed. At the moment, there are 6 other people in my room, and they are all engaging in an obscene conversation about past problems they have had with their genitals. Where am I? Anyways, today is the first day back in hostel after the 2-and-half-day "weekend" at home. When I returned to the hostel, I realized that I was among the earliest there. I wheeled my suitcases inside to meet the new house mother. Extending my hand, I introduced myself...we shook, but instead of saying, "Nice to meet you," or something of that sort, she immediately asked me why I was not in appropriate boarding house attire...I fought hard to not let this rude introduction make me sad and homesick all over again; after all, she doesn't seem nearly as bad as Ms. Johnson. Today there was—

Monday, November 20, 2006

6:20 pm (prep)

I did not get to finish what I was writing last night because the housemaster turned off the lights on us, causing me to have to fumble through the dark, back to my bunk. I had previously started writing, "Today there was..." What I was saying was that there was a huge party/gathering at Uncle's house that I wish I could have attended. Late Saturday evening, I witnessed 4 of Aunt Flora's friends come to the house and begin cooking for the festivities. They utilized MASSIVE cauldrons, and the food smelled so good.

That same evening, I had the opportunity to speak with you guys for over an hour. I'm so happy we talked, as it allowed me to forget so many of the stresses (concerning school and boarding house) that have been plaguing my mind. Shortly following, Uncle and I watched an entertaining movie on my laptop, which actually brought me an overwhelming sense of peace. It's interesting how a soul in distress can find comfort in things so simple; this undoubtedly is a clear example of how powerful the companionship of a family member can be. When Sunday morning came, the ladies resumed their cooking and only began to finish as I departed from the house to make my way back to hostel.

Today was not a bad day at all. Although I missed the first bus to school due to the new house mother making me change my black "trainers" (which also prevented me from being able to practice piano before school), I can't say that I was miserable. Mr. Alabi woke us all up by launching water in our faces this morning. This rude awakening made me sit straight up and rip the covers off my bed in annoyance. I sat there and stared at Mr. Alabi for over a minute—just glaring at him in defiance. Now that I think back upon the situation, I find it rather funny the way I reacted. The other boys simply screamed profanity when they were splashed, and I think one of them actually beamed his pillow at Mr. Alabi's head, narrowly missing him.

My chemistry teacher wasn't in school today, and the other chemistry teacher that I went to during recess didn't feel like answering my questions because he was eating his snack. Many teachers here are *excessively* lazy, which raises my stress level and forces me to seek a textbook reference that is rarely available. There are also certain times when the textbook is difficult to understand, but I have nobody reliable to answer my questions. Right now it is a quarter to 7, and the math teacher for "home-lessons" has arrived at the hostel. I'm the only one ready for his class, as everyone else is upstairs sleeping. I'll stop writing when he comes back into this wing of the dining room. I miss you guys and really wish you would send more emails to compensate for the small amount of time that we get to talk on the phone. The math teacher just came back...but he doesn't appear ready to teach anything...So as I was saying, I want to get emails on a daily basis. My goodness, I just spilled water all over myself. Bye!

Tuesday, November 21, 2006

8:27 am

Right now I am alone in the physics room and have an extremely sore throat. It actually feels more like the very rear of my nasal cavity, slightly above the back of my palette, is burning. I went to the hospital last night to get some antibiotics. This morning, the pain had increased by twice the amount. Mr. Alabi threw water on our faces this morning to wake us up. Everyone was extremely pissed, recoiling instantly and springing off their beds; however, he had to splash me 3 times before I got up, and when I was finally sitting upright, I pointed to my soaked pillowcase and asked him, "Are you happy now?"

While we were waiting for the first bus to take us to school, the person who arranged the dining room was carelessly tossing people's belongings around. I asked him to please not throw my bag off the table, and upon hearing this, one snotty, blackhearted year 9 boy (who everyone hates) then took it upon himself to fling it out the door. I got out of my chair, and walked up to the boy.

"Are you drunk?" I asked him.

In a blinding rage, I found my hands around his neck, pinning him to the wall and watching him struggle to break free for a good 10 seconds. I released him and collected my bag from outside. This is the way you must respond to minors who disrespect you in this country, or it will just keep happening...and not only will it keep occurring, but their transgressions will be bolder and more severe each time.

Wow, my throat is so sore. The reason I am in the physics room while assembly is taking place outside in the courtyard is because Madam Uko gave me a note to go and rest in the nurse's office, but the suite was *way* too hot. I asked to go upstairs to study (location of the science wing), knowing that they would have the air conditioning running. I really hope today is low-stress. It is now 8:40 am...By the way, I still haven't memorized Uncle's extremely long phone number, but I will make it a top priority when I return to the hostel after school.

5:15 pm (boarding house)

I just realized that my flash drive has been stolen. My devastation is indescribable; it had pictures of Micah and me, along with my entire personal journal stored on it. In distress, I composed a melody. It's quite bittersweet.

6:00 pm

I hope to high heavens that I get my flash drive back.

That's all I can think about right now. I found out at around 9:00 am this morning that my name had been called during the assembly I missed to receive an award for achievement in chemistry. This award recognizes me as a distinguished student with "drive and passion to achieve excellence." Can you believe that out of all the assemblies I could have missed, it just *had* to be this one??? This is the type of thing that makes me roll my eyes in disbelief.

By the way, last night when I went to the hospital, they took my height and weight measurements. According to the nurse, I am 179 cm tall and weigh 66.2 kg. About 5 minutes ago, I went into my schoolbag expecting to find my ruler that I could use to check the conversion of centimeters to inches, but to my dismay discovered that it was missing. I lent it out to one boy last night, and I suppose he "lost it," but I am determined to get it back. Within the first 2 weeks of school, all 25 pens that were supposed to last me the semester had been stolen. Sometimes I would get up from my desk to use the bathroom, and by the time I had come back to the classroom, all the utensils I had left out were gone. This is the type of behavior that causes me to refuse sharing my things with others, which inevitably generated a backlash of its own and earned me the name "selfish white prick." 24 hours a day, I am surrounded by thieves. I feel like I just can't win.

7:30 pm (prep)

Wow...the homework load in this school is dramatically less than at St. Mathicus. As a matter of fact, I typically finish all homework assignments within 30 minutes, but this doesn't include studying. On average, I find that I must study at least 3 hours daily. A few weeks ago it was more like 4.5 hours; however, now when reviewing my materials, I actually understand *everything* that I noted down in class. Stressing over every little detail in the beginning of the year has truly paid off. Thank you, God.

(PS) My throat still hurts quite a bit.

Wednesday, November 22, 2006

6:05 pm (prep)

Today I woke up with a sore throat once again. Is this medication working? Every day is the same, and it is really beginning to take a toll on me physically and mentally. Today I couldn't help but lament over my lacrosse skills that I feel slipping away from me with the inability to practice every day after school. When I think about how we would always practice our sports right after classes let out at St. Mathicus, I become extremely homesick. That was all I knew as an American child; however, in this school I am forced to sleep when I should be wind-sprinting up and down the football field! They call it siesta in this country. I call it misery. Sometimes I become terribly angry, as I can literally feel a cloud of laziness engulfing our everyday activities. Back at Uncle's compound, my soccer ball went over the fence. It has been 6 weeks and the neighbors on the other side of the 8-foot concrete wall still haven't given it back, so practicing soccer isn't even an option when I leave boarding house to go back home. Every time I ask if we can get a new ball, the answer is always along the lines of "eventually" or "maybe"...it simply doesn't matter to anybody.

A bunch of the other year 10s and I are performing a dance for the Christmas concert called "The Wolf Dance." We practiced after school today and are far from perfection. Following practice, there was an extremely agitating incident that occurred on the bus designated to take us back to hostel. Since it came 20 minutes early, I boarded just to drop my backpack off and greeted Mr. Alabi, who was sitting in the first passenger seat (because my upbringing has taught me that it's just the polite thing to do). He ignored me; however, as I proceeded to make my way back outside, he bellowed, "What are you doing boy?!" In other words, boarding the bus was supposed to restrict me from any further movement, and I wasn't allowed to run back up to the music room to collect my music books, which would probably be stolen by morning. Being accountable to this man 24/7 is dizzyingly frustrating! He is barcly literate and as a result finds arbitrary ways to flex his authority as a form of compensating.

On the bus ride home, our driver suddenly brought the bus to a stop. Nobody could put their finger on exactly what was going on until he got up from his seat and waddled his 300 lbs of pure muscle out the door and down the street; he was confronting a police officer. They began to argue, and from my point of view, it looked as if he was... hold that thought...*you know what?* Sometimes I get SICK OF THIS FREAKING COUNTRY!!! Mr. Alabi just came by and rudely switched off the A/C while I was in the middle of writing this entry! He saw that I was sweating bullets in front of the air conditioner, but he doesn't give a hoot because he is older than me and thus can do whatever he wants! This place is over 85 degrees, but I'm just a "little white boy," so who cares how I feel... Anyways...What I was writing before this wicked interruption was that it looked as if our bus driver was out for blood. He walked up to the police officer and clearly wanted to break his neck. I might stress once more that our bus driver is beastly looking enough to make you think he could lift the entire front end of the school bus; his forearms are tree-trunks. As soon as the driver got within striking distance of the officer, 4 people converged on him, restraining him by the neck, waist, and both arms. Surely this was for his own well-being, as the police over here shoot people indiscriminately with absolutely no accountability. Everyone on the bus was screaming and cheering the driver on, shouting, "Baddest guy!" "Big baba!" and "Kill em, now!" through the windows. I couldn't help but think of what could have transpired if they had actually engaged physically.

They don't have any pain medication in this hostel, and I am beginning to suspect that the doctor gave me placebo pills or simply the wrong type of antibiotics because my throat doesn't feel any better. Now that I think of it, he never looked me over in the first place. How did he actually know what my issue was? I would say it is probable that the entire trip to the hospital was in vain. All I can think of is the day I will be able to leave this wretched country and return to civilization. People here are extremely rude and self-centered. Drivers are a clear example of this, as they carelessly race through traffic and cut each other off. They don't have any traffic lights over here either, and on a daily basis there are dozens of accident-related deaths. In our school's snack shop called

"The Tuck Shop," kids desperately push and shove each other in line, as if gold is being dispensed in the front. When they get closer to the cashiers, everyone literally shoves their vouchers in the workers' faces, and I find it hard to imagine that they never make mistakes ringing up the wrong items. This country is lawless. There is no order.

Today I was sitting in class, talking to somebody, when all of a sudden a boy walked up and casually took the pen off of my desk. I saw him, but I didn't say anything because it would just be another reason for them to say, "See, you are just a stingy white man!" like they always do. Instead, I waited until after class to approach him and request my utensil back. He informed me that he had given it out to another person and lost track of it. This made me very unhappy.

Thursday, November 23, 2006

10:45 pm (inner room)

Wow. Today, life in boarding house was extremely hectic and rowdy. The year 9s are plotting to have a massive brawl against us year 10s. I specifically made it my business to not get involved in any way; however, it has been rather difficult trying to avoid 25 restless adolescents locked up in the same house. Earlier on, the physics teacher came to hostel to give us home lessons/"extra lessons," but I was the only person downstairs because everyone else was asleep. The plus to this was that we had a 1-on-1 lesson during which I was able to acquire many solutions to concepts I have been having difficulty in. My stomach is in knots with anxiety; I think I will go and read my Bible now.

Sunday, November 26, 2006

2:36 pm (prep)

Wow—looking back on the week, a lot of things have changed since Ms. Johnson left. First and foremost, there have been multiple fights on a daily basis between almost every member of this boarding house. I always stay away from fighting, but on Friday night I had to stand up for myself. One of the idiotic juniors came into my room and challenged me *in front of my peers* saying, "White fool, I'm in your face. Now what are you going to do about it?"

I unleashed the beast, backhanding him 3 times in his face and lifting him off his feet. He slammed into the wall and crawled backward in surprise. Nobody in the boarding house knew I was capable of striking another person, as in the past I have always avoided potential situations. Even in the wake of tonight's events they still haven't seen anything. They are in for a surprise. I've resolved to give them the brute force that they keep trying to elicit from me because at this point in boarding house, backing out of a fight will *literally* get you slapped around by your peers *and* juniors. That will NEVER happen to me.

To be honest, this boarding house is a zoo; late at night, you will hear screams and the sound of shifting bunk beds as the juniors rack (fight) one another. I've continued to excel academically, and just recently, socially to some extent. I know God is with me, as I can literally hear a voice inside me telling me where I should or shouldn't go, and when I should quickly do something in order to avoid trouble. Never in my life have I experienced anything of this nature before.

We will see who else fights tonight...I will pray and stay away as much as possible, but when physical conflict is inevitable, I will tear up my adversaries. I did not come here to be pushed around by lowlifes who have been expelled from multiple schools due to their inability to conduct themselves like decent human beings. May the Lord have mercy on the next jealous street fighter who wants to rack with me.

Argument

Monday, November 27, 2006

9:00 am

During today's assembly, I was awarded another certificate of achievement in chemistry.

Wednesday, November 29, 2006

9:20 am (Biology class)

Bio class was just cut short because a few of the custodians needed the chairs in our room for some sort of staff meeting. I'm not really complaining. We are now in the "assembly hall" without a teacher, just hanging out and talking. Physics class will take place in a short while, so I might as well study a little bit for that.

1:45 pm (Business Studies class)

This class is completely pointless—as I have expressed before. It is unfortunate that our teacher knows nothing and as a result struggles to dictate the textbook word for word while everyone laughs and screams at each other across the classroom (as usual). Might as well take this time to try and write another journal entry even though I probably won't be able to focus on it for long in this rowdy room.

I ended up having dance practice during physics class

and half of chemistry class this morning. I do not like the way dancing interferes with my core lessons. Falling behind makes things extremely challenging, and I have worked so hard just to keep on top of things so far.

5:40 pm (on bed, siesta)

Reminiscing upon yesterday's events, several of us boarding house students got together during recess to present our dire situation in hostel to Mrs. Wilson. This was one of the rare times that year 10s and 11s united for a common cause. We informed her of how Mr. Alabi would always come around with a bucket and throw water in our faces to wake us up in the morning, cut our snack portions in half, and deprive us of our tea that we are supposed to get before prep. We told her how he forces us to stay in bed against our will after school just because he declares it "siesta" and subtracts loaves of bread during Sunday morning breakfasts depending on his mood. It didn't end there; Mrs. Wilson soon learned of Mr. Alabi's habit of making arbitrary rules like forcing us to choose either jelly or butter for our morning toast, but not being allowed to have both. His decision to lock people out of prep for being late downstairs also came to light.

Later on that evening, we were called downstairs to have a follow-up meeting with the new house mother regarding our complaints. We were immediately confronted by Mr. Alabi, who accused us of being "rascals" but did little more. Sometimes you have to take matters into your own hands and deal with the repercussions.

So far today, we have not seen any retaliation from Mr. Alabi, but only time will tell.

Friday, December 1, 2006

3:00 pm (physics room)

Tonight is the long-anticipated year 10 dinner, where we dress up in suits and dine with the girls from our set in the school dining hall. You are supposed to have a date for the event, but I do not. I am currently waiting upstairs in the science wing, where several of my classmates and I have changed into our attire and casually *jist* (converse) back and forth about which girl we think is the prettiest. It's funny the way our school staff have isolated year 10s based on gender and homeroom; the entire evening seems to lack organization, as half of the boys are across the campus, while some of the girls are right across the courtyard. I suppose the aim is to keep students away from the hall while things are set up, but it is truly revolting when I compare America to the way things are haphazardly done over here. Mrs. Wilson has been a true lifesaver—you see, I didn't have a suit to wear for tonight's dinner in the first place. All the other kids in my grade either live locally or have parents in the area who were able to deliver their attire to the boarding house last night. When Mrs. Wilson found this to be the case, she took it upon herself to bring her son's former *graduation* suit to school for me to wear. It fit perfectly...what a blessing this woman is.

The best thing that happened to me today was the discovery of my "stolen" flash drive in my backpack, neatly tucked into one of the small outer pockets. I remember thinking that the blazer burglar had probably taken it as well, seeing that they both went missing in the same week. I won't lie, my stress level has been through the roof, and I can't wait until it is time to go back to Uncle's house for

Christmas break. The fact that it will be an 87-degree Christmas with mosquitos no longer fazes me.

Sunday, December 3, 2006

1:45 am (upstairs hallway)

Around 20 minutes ago I was lying on my bed in the tranquility of my dark room, trying to fall asleep. I would normally be dreaming by this time, but for some reason tonight was sleepless for me. I was in deep thought, when all of a sudden the door began to creak open. I heard whispers and what sounded like several feet tiptoeing across the floor. Immediately suspicious, I looked up and made out the silhouettes of many year 9 students, 2 of whom were carrying a large bed sheet. In the background, I saw the muscular frame of Nnamdi, who appeared to be issuing instructions to them. I watched in silence as they came to a stop in front of one of my sleeping classmates, Femi G. He was the scrawniest boy in my set and also happened to be extremely rude. Then I heard one of them whisper "1... 2... 3," and suddenly the sheet was cast over Femi as they proceeded to beat him mercilessly out of his sleep. About 10 seconds later, they were running out of the room, exploding in muffled laughter.

Femi moaned in pain, but not loud enough to wake anybody across the room, or even his bunkmate; I could tell that he was bleeding, but he decided to lay back down...which actually depressed me. 5 minutes later the door opened again; I immediately sat upright on my bunk, tensing every muscle in my body; however, they didn't actually notice me, as they were making their way into the inner room.

I heard them whispering, "Mofeayo next!" the full name of the mentally challenged boy from England who we all called Mofe. "Give it to Mofe!" one of them hissed excitedly.

By that time, over 15 year 9s had stealthily packed into the inner room, ready for action. Out of sight, all I heard was the unanimous sounds of fists pounding into flesh, followed by a startled cry.

"What the hell!" Mofe had begun screaming in a thick British accent. "What are you doing, fam? Get off me please! *Abeg jare* (please, please). GET OFF."

Once again, all the perpetrators ran out of our room. Now that they had beaten the two most unpopular kids in hostel, I knew I was next. Nnamdi was the ringleader, and he did not like me at all. Sure enough, about 3 minutes later, the door creaked open and I saw a couple of figures drop down low to the ground on all fours. I heard, "Get white boy. Beat him well," whispered in an eager voice. I pretended to be asleep until the last minute, and as the figures neared my bunk, I didn't hesitate: I jumped to my feet, ready to fight for my life and destroy anything in my path. The boys who were only inches away from me rose to their feet and jumped back, startled and confused.

Nnamdi's voice emerged in the background. "Hit him, hit him, hit him! Don't waste time, now!"

Despite his commands, the boys were frozen in front of me. Nnamdi pushed 2 more of them toward me in an attempt to provoke an attack.

Then one of them mocked, "This is it, white boy! You're done for!"

But nobody tried anything. They had apparently

realized it was not going to be as easy to beat me standing up as it would be if I had been asleep, according to plan. My mind was racing, and I was ready for war.

"Get out of my room, Satan," I growled.

They eventually retreated, but only once I aggressively advanced toward them. After everyone left the room, I armed myself with a belt and lay back down on my cot without any desire to sleep. I couldn't help but think of what would have happened to me had I been asleep. By this time, a few boys in my room were awake, but most were still asleep. I had a feeling they were not done, however, and 10 minutes later, just as I suspected, they walked in again (more boldly), but past my corner and straight up to Mofe for round 2. They brushed him again, but this time one of the year 11s woke up and began cursing at them. They ran away and didn't return for the rest of the morning.

This hostel is absurdly treacherous. Did I come to this country to be punished in this manner? What in the world is happening in my life right now?

Let's do a brief recap of the day: at 11:15 am, while everybody waited angrily for Saturday morning breakfast, Nnamdi and I were engaging in an endurance game that he introduced me to. The two people playing were to punch each other in the arms until somebody gave up. One of my hits rattled him hard, to which he became enraged and tried to lift me off my feet. I resisted as he began trying to grab my neck, at which point I realized that it was no longer a playful situation.

"What's wrong with you man?! What are you doing?!" I yelled.

He used this element of surprise to throw me into one

of the cots, where he attempted to slam me in the face, only succeeding in hitting my arms, which I had learned to keep guard in front of my head. From there, he threw me into the side of a bunk, where I hit my nose on the cold metal bar. I instantaneously decided this would never happen again, leaving the room.

That evening at 9:10 pm, I made my way upstairs and had just entered my room when I came face to face with Nnamdi, challenging me for round 2. I declined, but he followed me around the entire room, poking me and prodding me every few steps. Just when I thought things couldn't get any worse, he pulled a pin out of his pocket and pushed it into my backside. I didn't know what to do at this point, so I quickly ran downstairs and attempted to confide in Mr. Alabi.

After I had finished explaining the situation to him, the man whimsically asked me, "So what do you want me to do?"

I couldn't believe it. Instead of even pretending to care about what had been happening to me, he was mocking me! I sat there, stone cold for about 30 seconds, not knowing what to do or say. I was truly alone, and there was no denying it at this point. Enraged, I flew back up the stairs, into my room and proceeded to blow past Nnamdi; I was going to attempt to collect my things for showering. To my surprise, he did not try to fight me again, and that is what I am grateful for. Wow.

I cannot believe I have to wake up for church in 5 hours...Better try to get some sleep.

Saturday, December 9, 2006

6:00 pm (on my bed)

We are having socials right now, which is a 90-minute block that comes once a week (on Saturdays). This is the only time we are allowed to watch the 24-inch television in the prep/dining room. It is also the only time during which we are permitted to call our parents or play soccer outside; however, soccer is not an option at this time because Mr. Alabi is in a bad mood and is stashing the ball under his bed. I am so depressed that all I want to do is sit on my bed and write my pain away. All day we have been forced to sleep, and to be honest, every day is the same: absolutely uneventful torture. This lifestyle takes away my strength, athleticism, and talent. I often weep out of intense frustration, choosing the shower as a place to do so because the water disguises the tears flowing down my face. Why the *hell* am I subjected to a lazy man's schedule? God, please help me! I have worked so hard to obtain the incredible talents that are now slipping away from my body, and it feels like a slow, excruciating death!

Every day I beg God to allow me to play professional lacrosse when I return to the States, but I just end up with a terrible sinking feeling in the pit of my stomach because my common sense tells me it won't be possible. I am not afforded any opportunity to practice my sport! I HATE THIS LIFESTYLE! All we do in this God-forsaken place is eat, sleep, and schoolwork; it is causing me to gain weight! I have never had a physical problem of this nature before, which just adds to my stress. I cannot allow this to continue! Wouldn't you think that going back to Uncle's house would allow me to at least practice my soccer skills? It should, but think again because we do not have a soccer ball anymore, and although I have begged Auntie and Uncle to buy another one, no action has been taken. Everything is always put off until later, and this is a problem I have observed with closer to 85% of the Nigerians I have met over here. I can't stand it.

Compounding matters, new material in chemistry has me petrified because I have missed multiple lessons due to the mandatory Christmas show dance practices that I was drafted for. I never signed up to dance in the first place, and I certainly do not see how it is going to help me graduate high school. Mommy, you called 30 minutes ago, and I was filled with relief, coupled with the intense desire to tell you every last detail of what goes on over here. We were in the middle of our conversation when all of a sudden the phone line was cut; my heart dropped through the floor. I pleaded with that stupid Mr. Alabi man (who never showers or wears deodorant) to please retrieve the phone adaptor from his room, but he began yelling at me in a thick, barbaric accent. I looked into his yellowed eyes and had more disdain for him than ever before. I miss you guys, and I really miss freedom.

(PS) Today I composed another song. At least the music in my head is enjoyable.

Sunday, December 10, 2006

12:35 pm (on my bed)

The top of my left ear has been brutally severed, and the left side of my head is significantly swollen. This is how it happened:

Last night at around 11:45 pm, our room was extremely

hot, so out of desperation I walked into the inner room to sit next to the A/C.

I had only been there for around 30 seconds when I heard a voice snarl, "Get out, stupid white boy."

I looked up, and 5 feet from the adjacent bunk, I saw Bolaji's angry face contorted into a shockingly unsightly frown. I simply ignored him at first, but upon seeing that I was not taking the bullying, he repeated himself with a raised voice.

I turned to Bolaji and informed him that I was not there to disturb anyone but just needed to cool down before bed. "We all have to share the boarding house because we live together," I stated.

Turning my head away from him, I saw him get up and approach in my peripheral vision. Before I knew what was happening, my head was spinning and my left eye went blank; he had punched me directly in the temple. I gradually rose to my feet from the chair I was sitting in, fearing the prospect of striking him back. Slowly, I walked to the mirror in the middle of the room and proceeded to inspect myself. Bolaji followed me closely.

"Do you want more, whitey?" he shouted.

I defiantly faced him, "Are you going to hit me again?"

He immediately punched my face a second time. I was more than fed up. I threw an enormous punch at him, which he skillfully dodged. I stumbled backward and ran out of the room, Bolaji hot on my trail. I managed to pick up a heavy oak chair from the end of the laundry table outside the room, flinging it in the direction of his head with all of my adrenaline-fueled might. Unfortunately (or fortunately) the chair clipped the doorframe in which he was standing, fragmenting into several sharp, tiny pieces and simultaneously putting a massive dent in the door.

I proceeded downstairs to report to the house mother, who I knew liked Bolaji more than me. She was already halfway up the stairs.

"What is all the commotion about?" she hissed. She had only heard a little bit of my story before informing me that my ear was bleeding very badly; blood had begun flowing down the left side of my head.

I began telling her everything, as year 10s and seniors started to gather at the top of the stairs. Upon mentioning Bolaji's name as the instigator of the fight, the popular year 10 bully Omari interrupted me with a heinous lie.

"Bolaji was only defending himself."

This fib was too much for me to handle. "Omari, you were not even in the room," I snapped.

Omari had successfully caused the house mother to be unsure of who to believe, but there was far more evil to be spoken of the whitest boy in boarding house.

Kwasi approached the staircase and contributed, "Andrew threw a chair at Bolaji."

I couldn't believe my ears. Kwasi was so afraid of being bullied by Omari and Bolaji that he catered to their evil agenda without even knowing the full story. The house mother suddenly made up her mind to believe the growing majority, and although I was the only person visibly injured, she asked me if I expected her to believe me or the 3 other "witnesses" who were testifying against me. I tried to reason with her, but she barked at me, "Shut up!" She took me to the prep room downstairs to put spirit on the ear, which appeared to be severed one-fourth of the way off. 30 minutes later, I was on my way to a local hospital that did not have any electricity.

I waited alone in a dark waiting room to be treated. Over 90 minutes passed. I couldn't figure out what was taking so long, as there were no other patients around. A hospital staff member eventually took me to a room full of candles and a few fluorescent lanterns, where I received what was claimed to be a tetanus shot. The three nurses who were attending to me were extremely lazy, and I eventually found out that they had been sleeping while I was in the waiting room earlier on. The entire ordeal lasted until 3:00 am.

Another traumatic incident occurred last night prior to the altercation with Bolaji: I was called "*ole*" for taking bread from the kitchen. A brief background on the term "*ole*": since Nigeria is a country in which law is not effectively enforced by the state, punishment for criminal activity resides in the hands of the people. In the marketplace, when a thief is caught, he is labeled "*ole*" and receives a methodical execution on the spot. The first stage is beating the *ole* to within inches of their life. The next step is covering them from head to toe in kerosene. The third and final step is lighting fire to the kerosene and watching the thief slowly cook to death while chanting, "*Ole!*"

Taking bread from the kitchen is a common boarding house crime that always yields immense appreciation from your ravenous peers upstairs. I had never stolen anything before (and considering that our school fees paid for the food in boarding house, this wasn't actually stealing). I was desperate for a way to make my peers like me. I knew that the entire boarding house glared menacingly at me during Monday and Wednesday dinners when I was the only person served rice and stew. Since they were all forced to eat the disgusting *amala* soup with *eba* and *fufu*, I thought that maybe hand-delivering bread to them after prep would lessen the animosity I constantly experienced.

At around 9:30 pm, I saw that I had a real opportunity to make something happen. Since I was on "water filler" duty with two other boys named Nicholas and Saubauna, I had constant access to the inner kitchen until our job was complete. I quickly organized a plan of action with the other two boys. 5 minutes later, I was carrying a laundry basket with a few towels into the kitchen while Saubauna was attempting to distract Yaseyi, the disgustingly grumpy older cook who hated giving us what we needed from the kitchen. Yaseyi would always give me problems when I requested more food and treated the boarding house kitchen as if it was her own kingdom that you were to consider yourself privileged to have access to. I targeted the 20-something loaves of bread, sitting upon the horizontal meat freezer and slowly approached. I coughed loudly as I knocked a loaf into the basket and quickly covered it with the towels. I excitedly made my way upstairs, brought out the bread, and hid it under my bed; Nicholas and I would decide when it was the appropriate time to dispense. *The boys in my room are going to be thrilled!* I thought ecstatically. I went back downstairs and successfully repeated the same process, but on my way back up the stairs this time, I found Mr. Alabi patrolling suspiciously close to the laundry table. I decided it would be best to place the laundry basket containing the second loaf with the other baskets next to the ironed school shirts and go back downstairs.

By the time I had decided to return upstairs, I was hearing a loud discussion between Mr. Alabi and Yaseyi, who had just discovered the absence of the two loaves of bread from the kitchen. *Did she really count all of them?* I thought to myself. I immediately changed direction to avoid them, but upon hearing my name "ANDEHROO!" shouted, I walked innocently up to him to ask what was wrong. "Follow me!" he ordered. Mr. Alabi led me outside, where we stood directly next to one of the external entrances of the kitchen. He accused me of taking the bread. By the time I had started denying it, Nicholas and Saubauna had already rushed down the stairs screaming "thief!" In under 90 seconds, the entire hostel had emptied, encircling me outside chanting, "*Ole!*" I couldn't believe my ears, nor could I believe what followed: people started poking and prodding me from all different angles, while others tried half-heartedly to knock me off my feet. I attempted to view it as playful; however, Nnamdi took the opportunity to punch me hard in the back, retreating into the crowd before Mr. Alabi could see him.

When almost everybody had gone back into the boarding house, I asked Mr. Alabi if we could have a private conversation. He led me to a room on the opposite side of the boarding house complex. I proceeded to tell him the truth: whenever we are having a meal that I cannot tolerate (*eba, fufu, moinmoin*), I am given rice or bread. As a result of this "special treatment," many of the boarding house bullies greatly resent me, and when it comes to mealtime, I find several people staring at me in pure hatred. Bread has been taken from the kitchen on many occasions by my classmates; however, when it is brought back upstairs, I am always the only one excluded from the spoils. In the event that I make the mistake of asking to partake in the festivities, everybody yells, "Ah-ah!?" and I hear names like "greedy white pig" or "stupid yellow man" screamed across the room. During our tea time right before prep, whoever is assigned tea server makes sure to give me a half-cup of tea, while topping everybody else's mug off. There is a ton of fighting in the hostel, and in order to avoid being a continual target, I decided to do something that would yield me appreciation from my envious peers. I am completely alone. I need an ally. I am sick and tired of being labeled selfish just because I don't split my dinner in half to feed the 3 other boys who always ask me for my food during Tuesday night meals. They have a huge plate of their own food! It always ends in name calling such as "white, rich American boy." This time around, the attempt to do good backfired horrendously, and Nicholas and Saubauna (the same boys who planned everything with me) turned on me and accused me of stealing the bread for myself, with no intent of sharing!

Mr. Alabi listened in silence. I could tell that my story was not going to garner any sympathy from him.

End of Diary

That night as I lay in bed reminiscing about the bread incident hours earlier, something inside me changed. I was no longer willing to tiptoe around the boarding house, trying to please my nasty peers and occasionally getting sucker punched in the process. I resolved to fight fire with fire. For the first time in my life, I faced the prospect of death like a man. I was now willing to die fighting. At least I would be remembered as a man and not a woeful coward.

Returning to school that week, looking like my face had been run over by a locomotive, I endured the laughter and jeers of Bolaji's friends. Bolaji pranced about the school with his head held high, knowing that everyone was looking at him with respect. He had made an example out of me. Every once in a while, I caught younger students staring at my black and blue face in pity.

For about ten days, I kept to myself, nursing my wounds and methodically planning my attack. Then the night came.

All the year 10s and year 11s were downstairs studying during the first prep period before dinner. Bolaji was in the corner of the room with his feet on the table, pretending to read as he dozed with the textbook covering his face, which was hidden from Mr. Alabi's view. I got up and pretended to get a drink from the water fountain a few feet from him. Adrenaline surged through my body, and my hands shook as I braced myself above the stream of water I pretended to drink. I turned around and slinked over toward him, acting like I was stretching. I twisted my entire torso so that my right hand came far behind my right leg. Then I untwisted my torso and rammed my clenched right fist into the side of Bolaji's neck. He flew off his chair.

The entire room rose to their feet as I hurled myself on top of him, sending punch after punch into his fat nose. I screamed, "Die! Die!"

Bolaji's friends quickly converged on me, restraining me on the floor. Bolaji was clearly dazed.

Mr. Alabi rushed into the room and stepped in between us, preventing additional blows.

"I'm going to kill you, white boy," Bolaji seethed. "Just you wait. Your parents are going to receive your pasty dead body in a trash bag."

I smiled at him defiantly, my face bruised and lacerated. As I looked into his eyes, I saw fear. I knew that attacking Bolaji wasn't going to make things better between us, but I also knew that it couldn't make life in boarding house worse. It was a step in the right direction. I'd finally proven myself a man in a prison-like setting where incivility was revered.

The next day in school, word spread like wildfire: "Andrew beat Bolaji." Several kids from my grade, who had never talked to me before, approached me to shake my hand. I could see that the only thing these people understood was brute force. What a shame. *How far I've fallen from my days at St. Mathicus,* I mused as a bitter wave of depression and nostalgia washed over me.

The next seven days were refreshingly peaceful, but something in me had changed: I wanted more violence. I did 400 pushups a day, cramming them into every free moment I find. I was training my body and preparing my mind for my next fistfight. I didn't know when it would occur, but I knew exactly how I would dodge, block, and jab.

On the eighth day after my fight with Bolaji, a boy named Ore started mocking the way I was speaking at dinner time.

"This guy, why do you sound like a stupid white fool from America's safest city?" he asked me.

As I studied my opponent, I took note of a few things: Ore had a flat chest but large triceps and biceps. Fighting him would be dangerous, but it wouldn't be impossible for me to win. I casually hurled a few curse words over the dinner table at him and continued eating as he responded with insults of his own. The tension in the air was almost palpable, and everybody knew that it was likely that Ore and I would get physical that night.

Twenty minutes later, we'd all migrated upstairs to the bedrooms to kill time until the beginning of second prep. Fifteen boys sat in my room, including Ore, who was lounging on his bunk bed a few feet from mine. He began to recall to everybody in the room the insults he'd flung at me over the dinner table. The room erupted in snickers.

"Shut up, Ore!" I snapped.

Ore got up and walked to my bed, where I was lying down. He got so close to me that his crotch was touching my elbow. Adrenaline began coursing through my veins, and I pulled myself into a seated position and calmly rose to my feet.

Grinning, Ore said, "This guy, what are you going to do? You're too scared to do anything, *abeg* nothing dey happen."

In a flash, the fight was on. I swung at Ore's teeth as hard as I could, but Ore deftly dodged my punch. Then he grabbed my chest and forced me into the wall with all his might. We exchanged blows, but I blocked each of his punched. When I landed a tremendous right hook to his nose, blood poured from his nose, drenching us both. Enraged, Ore put me in a headlock with a vise grip that seemed almost inescapable. By some miracle, I grabbed one of Ore's hands and bit viciously into the soft flesh between his thumb and index finger. I wanted to bite a hole into the meat of his hand.

He screamed in agony; the boys in the room roared in delight. Half of them cheered, "Break Andrew's head!' The other half encouraged me to remove Ore's eyes.

Mr. Alabi heard the bunk beds shifting from downstairs, and he burst into the room to break us up. I was injured, but Ore was mangled. I'd clearly won the fight. I sat back down on my bed as Mr. Alabi led Ore downstairs, scolding him for bothering me.

It took a long time to get my heart rate back to normal. I felt proud, dangerous, and depressed all at once.

The next day before school, I confronted Mofe. I asked

him in a gentlemanly way why he picked on me when I was one of the only people in school who didn't mock him for being in special classes. I asked him if he thought starting an altercation with me had boosted his social rank in boarding house. Mofe spent his entire schooldays reading comic books and tracing and color-in superheroes, and I knew that his pencils were his weakness. I ripped his backpack off his shoulders and emptied it onto the ground. Then I methodically broke each an every pencil. His eyes were wide as he watched my nimble hands snap one pencil after another.

"What the hell, Andrew?!" he wailed.

I calmly removed my shoes, then I used them to pound his face as hard as I possibly could. I beat him for what seemed like five minutes. His blood stained my pressed school shirt, but I didn't care. I wore his blood to school like a badge of honor. What did I care what anybody there thought about me?

Lying in my bed that night, I wondered what had happened to me. I was no longer the preppy, lacrosse-loving skateboarder from a prestigious private school. I was a coarsened brute. Tears poured from my eyes. I just couldn't win. Fighting for my life in this den of jackals, I had lost myself. And I was beginning to hate the person I'd become.

Yearbook picture, surrounded by my bullies

Performing during the Christmas concert

10

STUPID GOAT

The more I reflected on all my fights, the more melancholic I became. I escaped in my diary and my textbooks. Mr. Alabi told me that he saw a clear change in my persona. I was reserved, and I ate less. My eyes were also devoid of joy. Around then, he began treating me less like an inmate and more like a son. He understood my plight, but he was careful to not let the other boys see how much he favored me.

Thanks to the seismic change in our relationship, the boarding house became more of a refuge than it had ever been. Though still extremely sad, I was now undoubtedly more comfortable there when I lay my head down to rest at night.

One day at school, I wrote to my mother this email:

Dear Mommy,

Looking at the Johns Hopkins University online application puts a huge knot in my stomach; I haven't done my SATs, nor do I feel confident that I will be able to formulate a concrete timeline for having them completed. Uncle and I haven't agreed on a specific date to sit for the exams, and if I don't become more assertive and aggressive over this urgent issue, I feel that the SATs will never get done. The SAT score reports are due on the 15th of December. I'm freaking out. What am I going to do?

By the way, Mom, when it comes to work experiences, honors, and extracurricular activities, I get a sense of how demanding Johns Hopkins University is. The problem is that I have almost nothing to show in these areas...so what should I do? Is there still time to be able to do the things I need to do? Are work experience, honors, and extracurriculars absolutely mandatory in order to be considered?

How is it even remotely conceivable that I would get into Hopkins or any Ivy League school if I don't have anything in these areas?

Sometimes I get so angry at Uncle because no matter how many times I ask him if I can go out and do something productive, the answer is always along the lines of "let's talk about it later." I spent all summer trapped in the house (usually without electricity) with that wretch, Flora. I never once left that house to go out and do anything. I feel as if I've been forgotten and forsaken. Left to waste away. I can't imagine anything I could do to regain the time I've lost. At schools like St. Mathicus, students are undoubtedly able to check all the honors and work experience boxes with ease, seeing that there are endless extracurricular opportunities provided by school.

I've lost my mind worrying. Please call me this Saturday.

I love you,

Drew

A month later, Mr. Alabi left boarding house forever. I felt like a victim in a horror movie. Every good thing that ever came my way was immediately ripped from my hands. Nothing positive lasted.

Mr. Alabi's replacement was one of the most sadistic, twisted men I've ever met. Mr. Abioye was an extremely dark-skinned teacher who was infamous for spanking students on stage during assembly. He and I had never interacted much outside of the polite, "Good afternoon, sir," which I offered when passing him in the hallways. I had no idea how much disdain he secretly harbored for me.

Mr. Abioye ran the boarding house like a tyrant. If he caught people sleeping during prep, he poured a bucket of water on their faces, soaking their books and sending them crashing to the floor. But nobody endured more of Mr. Abioye's wrath than I did.

My trouble with Mr. Abioye began one night during dinner, when he started pestering me about eating rice.

"Andrew, do you think you are special?" he asked, sounding almost whimsical.

"Sorry, sir? I don't understand the nature of the question," I responded.

"Why must you insist on eating rice while all your peers eat *eba*? Heeeey, my brotha, you truly are a white king." He bowed down beside me, then he got on one knee. Everybody in the dining room stared, and I could see their hatred for me being rekindled, which was exactly what Mr. Abioye wanted.

I remained silent, refusing to meet his gaze.

"You don't want to face me, eh? I am your Black servant, Andrew. You are my king. Do you understand?"

I ignored him. He rose from his knee and knocked my plastic cup of water off the table.

"*Yepa!*" exclaimed several of the boys, apparently shocked by his brazenness.

"Oops. I'm sorry, my king. You need to wash that cup now. As a matter of fact, do me a favor and assume kitchen duty for the night," said Mr. Abioye.

I glared at him. "Why are you bullying me? Aren't you supposed to be a mentor, protector, and role model?" I snapped.

Mr. Abioye grinned slyly, and in a soft voice said, "Oh, boy. You don't know what you have done to yourself at this time."

"What are you talking about? You're not making sense! You come over here and make fun of me for eating the food I've been eating for over a year. Then you smack my cup off the table and put me on kitchen duty! What did I ever do to you?!" I shot back.

"You stupid, filthy, stuck-up, Caucasian goat!" he bellowed. "God has punished your mother with your existence. You will see who you are dealing with in this place, I tell you!" he spat before storming off into his room, slamming the door behind him.

Some of the boys exclaimed, "*Chai!* This guy, you dey mess up, oh!" (Wow, dude, you've messed up)

I suspected I was now on Mr. Abioye's bad side, but I had no idea how much worse it was about to get for me.

After dinner, I obediently assumed kitchen duty alone, cleaning the entire boarding house's plates, cups, and cutlery for a good two hours. I prayed for deliverance the entire time, not that those prayers did me much good. Although duties in boarding house rotated every week, Mr. Abioye would put me on kitchen duty for weeks at a time.

. . .

One day weeks later, Mr. Abioye identified my boxers on the clothesline after I'd spent an hour washing my undergarments. He walked to the clothesline and threw my boxers on the dirt floor. The third time he did it, I decided to hang my dripping boxers from the metal bars of the top bunk bed, which meant that my mattress and sheets were damp at all times. That made sleeping that much more uncomfortable. Because Mr. Abioye couldn't find my boxers on the clothesline anymore, he began throwing my bath towel on the bathroom floors near the urinals. He was a sadist posing as an educator.

I was afraid that reporting Mr. Abioye to the principal would only make matters worse, but after one particularly bad night, I decided that I had no other choice. That night, I'd begun to doze off during prep. I hadn't slept well for the past several days because the house was hot and humid. Rather than dumping a bucket of water on me, Mr. Abioye yanked the cords from behind the television, snuck over to me, and began savagely whipping my back.

I screamed and jumped to my feet. "What the hell?!"

He looked me in the eye and whipped me one final time, this time across my chest. "What, are you going to fight me now?"

I threw my textbook into the ceiling fan, then I hurled my backpack across the room, narrowly missing one of my classmates. I stormed away toward my bedroom.

"Typical temper tantrum from a spoiled white brat!" Mr. Abioye yelled after me. "Your new name is SOD! That stands for son of the Devil."

The next day in school, I reported Mr. Abioye's abusive behavior to the principal and the headmaster. I'm sure they warned him, but that night in hostel, that wasn't obvious. As soon as we returned from school, Mr. Abioye made me kneel down on the stones outside for an hour. I felt as though my knees were being slowly shattered, which made me break into a sweat. Whenever I attempted to shift some of the weight off my knees, he yelled from the window, "SOD, that is cheating. I shall restart your time if you continue the tomfoolery!"

The next morning at 5:30, he didn't wake us by shouting at us, which was his usual method. Instead, Mr. Abioye crept into our room with a keg full of water and poured water directly into my nostrils. I woke up terrified, choking and coughing.

He smiled. "SOD, it's time to get up." Then he yelled at the rest of the room.

Every day for the next week, Mr. Abioye poured water on my face at 5:30 am. As a result, I became an extremely light sleeper, and I learned to wake up at the sound of our bedroom door opening. The first day that I woke up before he could try to drown me in my sleep, he splashed me in the face and whispered, "Wake up, white SOD."

I rose to my feet and shouted in his face, "I'm already awake, Mr. Abioye! Do you think God doesn't see your wickedness? Do you think that you're immune from his wrath or that justice won't be served? Go ahead, make my life hell for the remaining weeks that I'm here in this miserable, malaria-ridden jungle! Just remember that I'll move back to the States and never return to this prison, but you'll spend the rest of your days in this hellhole, rejoicing whenever there's half-current electricity and bathing in typhoid water!"

My rant turned a room full of dozing zombies into wide-awake spectators. Mr. Abioye stood silently in front of my bed, the keg of water swishing at his side. Then he turned and left without saying another word to anybody.

My life there couldn't get any worse, so I didn't care.

I spent the next few weeks before graduation with my head down, stoically enduring whatever arbitrary task the demonic man demanded of me. Phone calls to Uncle or to my parents weren't an option for me anymore because I'd been permanently banned from using the telephone in boarding house, and I never had an opportunity to make a call at school.

On the day of graduation, Mr. Abioye found me in school and told me that I wouldn't be allowed to attend the graduation ceremony because I wasn't performing tasks in boarding house to his satisfaction. I laughed in his face and asked him if he wanted to fight me. Then I graduated.

Graduation ceremony

Standing next to one of the bullies who beat me in the past

Posing with a teacher

That same week of graduation, I moved back to Uncle Arnold's house for the last time. I was happy to be reunited with him and Auntie Adamma. I knew that Auntie's sister, Flora, wasn't going to congratulate me, but I hadn't anticipated that she'd outright ignore my presence. In the days before my flight back to the United States, Flora made sure I was uncomfortable in the house. She hid all the TV remotes and locked the kitchen at night to prevent me from freely accessing food. She also locked the storage to prevent me from accessing toiletries. I didn't have the energy to complain to Uncle or Auntie about the bitter woman. I couldn't fathom the iciness of her stone-cold heart, but I took solace in the fact that I'd be home soon.

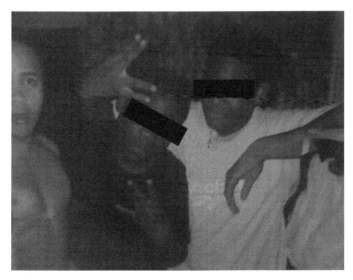

Roommates

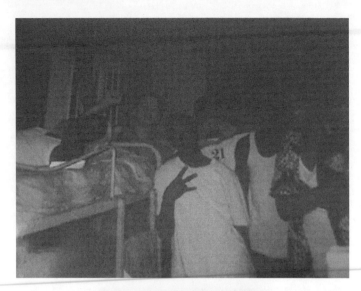

Left to right: Micah and me

EPILOGUE
WELCOME HOME

Back in Baltimore for the first time in more than two years, I got off the plane and took in the crisp, clean air. It was about seventy degrees—perfect. A dopamine rush overwhelmed me. It occurred to me that I could use a cell phone for the first time in years. I could get whatever I needed by simply driving to the local store. And I had electricity and potable water again. Making my way through the boarding bridge, I cried for joy.

Mommy walked right past me in the terminal because she didn't recognize me. I'd transformed from a meek, skinny boy into a broad-shouldered, bearded, African man.

"Mommy!" I called to her.

She gasped. I held her tightly and told her how much I loved her. Micah and Daddy stood close behind her, both grinning broadly, ecstatic to see me. Micah had sprouted more than a foot. I picked him up and asked him who he thought he was, growing taller than me.

"My baby is home," said my father in a soft, proud voice. He pulled me into his muscular chest and held me firmly.

I soaked up every ounce of Daddy's gentle strength.

. . .

The roads in Baltimore were unnervingly smooth—no bus-swallowing potholes on the route home. I hadn't experienced such a peaceful ride in years. The traffic was so orderly that it put me on edge. I feared that it was the calm before a terrible storm. Strangely, I worried about not being worried about the prospect of imminent death. My brain had become accustomed to perpetual fear.

That night, I went to a fast food restaurant for the first time in what felt like forty years. I ordered a cheeseburger, fries, chicken nuggets, and a milkshake. There was no limit to the number of items I could select from the menu. I could eat anything I wanted and as much of it as I wanted. And there was no time limit for my meal. I haphazardly downed half my burger before starting in on the nuggets. I crammed fries into my face and took inadvisable gulps of my milkshake. My brother and I howled with laughter the entire time.

After dinner, I visited the local superstore. The building was exquisite. This was no marketplace in the middle of a dirt field. I didn't have to brush flies off the produce, and I wasn't harried by honking flocks of rusted-out beaters, stuck in bumper-to-bumper traffic. I had a feeling that the store managers hadn't burned any thieves to death that day. I also suspected that the goods on the shelves weren't counterfeit. And best of all, the price of everything in sight was one-fourth of what it would be in Nigeria.

Then we got home, and I felt like I had walked into a five-star hotel. Our house was so clean. The electricity was running smoothly, and it wasn't likely to stop either. I'd forgotten the feeling of carpet on my feet—amazingly soothing. I took off my shirt and sprawled out on the cushy living room floor. I stared at the ceiling for about ten minutes, breathing in the wonderful, air-conditioned oxygen. Classical music played faintly on the kitchen radio. I hadn't heard that in a while. I got up and pranced into the kitchen. Turning on the sink, I bent down and gulped water that wouldn't give me typhoid. That seemed like a minor miracle.

I walked down the hallway toward my bedroom, hands pressed to the walls, appreciating the texture of the paint. My room was spotless—no dirt or sand on the floor, no malarial mosquitos lurking ominously in the corners. I leapt as high as I could and came crashing down on my soft mattress, belly first. I'd forgotten how comfortable a bed could be. I unboxed the new flip phone waiting for me on my headboard. I didn't know who to call, but I loved knowing that I could pick it up and use it whenever I felt the urge to reach out to someone.

Lying in my childhood bed felt surreal. *So this is what it's like to not be afraid in my own room*, I thought. No bully was going to charge in and threaten to beat me. Mr. Abioye wouldn't be whipping me with power cords for imagined infractions that night. And no longer would I have to worry about Flora calling her brothers to thrash the "white man." This was what home was supposed to feel like.

I was so glad that those days were behind me, but from a distance, I was also beginning to appreciate what they had done for me. My brutal experiences had armed me with resilience, strength, and confidence. Those traits would open doors for me. I'd use all of that negativity to build something lasting for myself.

I slept easy that night.

ABOUT THE AUTHOR

Drew is an IT professional and student at Johns Hopkins University, where he is pursuing his master's degree.

Made in the USA
Middletown, DE
17 July 2021